FEDERICO GARCÍA LORCA

The House of
Bernarda Alba

La casa de
Bernarda Alba

translated,
with commentary and notes by
GWYNNE EDWARDS

methuen | drama

LONDON • NEW YORK • OXFORD • NEW DELHI • SYDNEY

METHUEN DRAMA
Bloomsbury Publishing Plc
50 Bedford Square, London, WC1B 3DP, UK

BLOOMSBURY, METHUEN DRAMA and the Methuen Drama logo are trademarks
of Bloomsbury Publishing Plc

First published in Great Britain 1998 by Methuen Drama
Reissued with a new cover design by Bloomsbury Methuen Drama 2009
Reprinted 2010, 2011, 2013, 2014, 2015, 2016 (twice), 2017 (twice), 2018 (twice), 2019

A catalogue record for this book is available from the British Library.

ISBN: PB: 978-0-7136-8677-7
ePDF: 978-1-3501-5930-3
ePub: 978-1-3501-5929-7

A catalog record for this book is available from the Library of Congress.

Series: Student Editions

Typeset by Deltatype Ltd, Birkenhead, Merseyside

To find out more about our authors and books visit www.bloomsbury.com
and sign up for our newsletters.

Contents

Federico García Lorca: 1898–1936

1898 Born on 5 June in the village of Fuente Vaqueros in the province of Granada, the eldest of the four children of Don Federico García Rodríguez, a wealthy farmer and landowner, and Doña Vicenta Lorca Romero, a former schoolteacher in the village.

1907 The family moves to the village of Asquerosa, later called Valderrubio, only three miles from Fuente Vaqueros, where Don Federico buys a large house.

1908 Attends a boarding school in the town of Almería, some
–09 seventy miles from Granada, but his stay there is cut short by illness.

1909 Don Federico moves the family to Granada, the city which was to play such an important part in Lorca's work. He attends a small private school, the College of the Sacred Heart of Jesus, which, despite its name, is free of clerical influence. He is much more interested in music, in particular in playing the piano, than in his academic studies.

1914 After failing the second part of his final secondary education
–15 examinations in 1914, he retakes it successfully in the following year and, at the instigation of his parents, enters the Faculties of Philosophy and Letters and of Law at the University of Granada. His university career proves to be less than remarkable, but he comes under the influence of two distinguished professors: Martín Domínguez Berrueta, Professor of the Theory of Literature and the Arts, and Fernando de los Ríos Urruti, Professor of Political and Comparative Law. His musical abilities continue to develop under the teaching of Don Antonio Segura. He joins the Arts Club in Granada and also begins to frequent the Café Alameda, a meeting-place for the intellectuals and artists of the town, as well as for foreign visitors such as H. G. Wells,

Rudyard Kipling and Artur Rubinstein.

1916 Study trips in May and October, organised by Domínguez Berrueta, to various Spanish towns and cities.

1917 In the spring and summer two further study trips. Lorca begins to write poetry, prose and short plays. Much of the poetry is concerned with sexual love and reveals the conflict in his mind between sexual desire and Catholic sexual morality.

1918 With the financial assistance of his father, Lorca publishes *Impressions and Landscapes*, a book based on his earlier travels with Domínguez Berrueta.

1919 In Granada meets Gregorio Martínez Sierra, a Madrid theatre producer, who encourages him to write a play about an injured butterfly (*The Butterfly's Evil Spell*), and the great Spanish composer, Manuel de Falla, with whom he begins an influential friendship. Moves from Granada to Madrid, commencing a ten-year stay at the Residencia de Estudiantes, an educational institution based on the Oxbridge college system. Meets Luis Buñuel, the future film director, who had entered the Residencia in 1917.

1920 *The Butterfly's Evil Spell* premieres at the Teatro Eslava in Madrid on 22 March but closes after four performances. Audience hostility towards a play about cockroaches, a butterfly and a scorpion is accompanied by poor reviews.

1921 Publication in Madrid of Lorca's first volume of poetry, *Book of Poems*.

1922 Completes a play for puppets, *The Tragicomedy of Don Cristóbal and Señorita Rosita*. In February Lorca lectures on 'deep song' (flamenco song) at the Arts Club in Granada, and, with Manuel de Falla and Miguel Cerón, helps to organise the Festival of Deep Song, held on 13 and 14 June in the Alhambra's Plaza de los Aljibes. In anticipation of these events, he had written in the previous year a series of poems inspired by 'deep song' which he hoped to publish in conjunction with the festival.

1923 Organises with Manuel de Falla a puppet show which includes Lorca's own puppet play, *The Girl who Waters the Basil Plant*, and which takes place on 6 January in the García Lorcas' large flat in Granada. In the same month Lorca completes his law degree. In the Residencia he embarks on his important friendship with Salvador Dalí.

1924 Works on a collection of poems, *Gypsy Ballads*, on his second full-length play, *Mariana Pineda*, and on another play strongly influenced by the puppet tradition, *The Shoemaker's Wonderful Wife*. At the Residencia he becomes friendly with Rafael Alberti, who would soon become one of Spain's leading poets.

1925 Stays with Salvador Dalí and his sister, Ana María, at the family homes in Cadaqués and Figueras. Reads *Mariana Pineda* to them. Visits and is much impressed by Barcelona. Back in Granada writes several short plays, of which *Buster Keaton's Spin* and *The Maiden, the Sailor and the Student* survive.

1926 Completes *The Love of Don Perlimplín for Belisa in his Garden*. In Granada he delivers an important lecture, 'The Poetic Image in Don Luis de Góngora', on the great seventeenth-century Spanish poet. Publishes *Ode to Salvador Dalí*.

1927 Premiere of *Mariana Pineda*, to great acclaim, on 24 June at the Teatro Goya in Barcelona. Lorca exhibits twenty-four of his drawings at the Galerías Dalmau in the same city. Publishes *Songs*, his second volume of poems. *Mariana Pineda* opens at the Teatro Fontalba in Madrid on 12 October and is enthusiastically received.

1928 Edits the first issue of the literary magazine, *Cockerel*. He becomes involved with a young sculptor, Emilio Aladrén, to whom he is passionately attracted. At the end of July *Gypsy Ballads* is published to great critical acclaim, but is criticised by Dalí and Buñuel for being too traditional and not sufficiently avant-garde. During the summer Lorca feels depressed. In the autumn he delivers two lectures to the Athenaeum Club in Granada, 'Imagination, Inspiration and Escape in Poetry', and 'Sketch of the New Painting'.

1929 The Madrid premiere of *The Love of Don Perlimplín for Belisa in his Garden* is banned by the authorities. On 29 April *Mariana Pineda* opens triumphantly at the Teatro Cervantes in Granada. Emilio Aladrén begins to be involved romantically with the English girl he would marry two years later. This, together with anxieties about his deteriorating relationship with Dalí and about his work and his growing fame, exacerbates Lorca's depression. His family decide to send him to New York in the company of Fernando de los Ríos, where, after visiting Paris, London, Lucton School near Ludlow, Oxford, and Southampton, he arrives on 19 June. Enrols as a student of English at Columbia University, visits Harlem, then spends the summer in Vermont before returning to New York. Witnesses the Wall Street Crash. Works on *Poet in New York* and writes *Trip to the Moon*, a screenplay for the silent cinema, inspired in part by a visit to Coney Island but expressing too his own sexual anxieties.

1930 Leaves New York for Cuba, arriving in Havana on 7 March. Works on *The Public* and on *Ode to Walt Whitman*. Returns to Spain at the end of June. *The Shoemaker's Wonderful Wife* premiered in Madrid at the Teatro Español on 24 December.

1931 Publication of *Poem of Deep Song*. Completes *When Five Years Pass*. Appointed by the new left-wing Republican government as the artistic director of the Teatro Universitario, a touring theatre group which came to be known as 'La Barraca'. For the next four years the company would perform the great Spanish plays of the sixteenth and seventeenth centuries in the towns and villages of rural Spain as part of the government's broad-based educational programme.

1932 Lorca works on *Blood Wedding*. Reads *Poet in New York* in Barcelona.

1933 Premiere of *Blood Wedding* on 8 March at the Teatro Beatriz in Madrid, acclaimed by all the critics. *The Love of Don Perlimplín for Belisa in his Garden* premiered at the Teatro Español in Madrid on 5 April. Lorca works on *Yerma* and in October travels to Argentina where he both lectured and attended productions of his own plays: *Blood Wedding* and *The Shoemaker's Wonderful Wife*, both triumphantly received in Buenos Aires.

1934 *Mariana Pineda* opens in Buenos Aires on 12 January but receives only lukewarm reviews. Lorca's adaptation of Lope de Vega's *The Foolish Lady* is specially performed for an audience of actors. He arrives in Spain once again on 11 April and recommences work with 'La Barraca'. The bullfighter Ignacio Sánchez Mejías, a close friend of Lorca, receives fatal wounds in the bullring in Manzanares on 11 August. Shortly afterwards Lorca begins writing *Lament for Ignacio Sánchez Mejías* and also works on *Doña Rosita the*

Spinster. On 29 December *Yerma* opens at the Teatro Español in Madrid. Despite an attempt by the Right to disrupt the performance, the play is received with great enthusiasm by both audience and critics.

1935 *The Shoemaker's Wonderful Wife* opens at the Madrid Coliseum on 18 March. Publication of *Lament for Ignacio Sánchez Mejías*. *The Puppet Show of Don Cristóbal* performed in the Paseo de Recoletos during the Madrid Book Fair. Lorca's version of *The Foolish Lady* is performed in both Madrid and Barcelona. *Yerma* opens in Barcelona on 17 September. Lorca works on *Sonnets of Dark Love* and on *Play Without a Title*. *Blood Wedding* opens in Barcelona on 22 November at the Principal Palace Theatre, to be followed by the triumphant premiere, on 12 December, of *Doña Rosita the Spinster*.

1936 Increasing political trouble in Spain. The Right and Centre parties defeated by the left-wing Popular Front in the February General Election. In the following months Lorca's socialist sympathies are increasingly in evidence. Publishes *Six Galician Poems* and *First Songs*. Works on *The Dreams of My Cousin Aurelia*, *Blood Has No Voice* (now lost), and *Play Without a Title*. Rehearsals of *When Five Years Pass* for a production at the Anfistora Club. *The House of Bernarda Alba* is completed on 19 June and in the following week reads the play to groups of his friends. Political unrest continues and Lorca leaves Madrid for Granada on 13 July. Five days later Franco initiates a military uprising against the Madrid government. The military in Granada rise on 20 July. Lorca, fearing the worst, takes refuge in the house of a fellow poet and friend, Luis Rosales. He is taken away from there on 16 August and detained in the Civil Government building. In the early hours of 18 August he is driven by Francoist thugs to a building outside the village of Víznar, north-east of Granada. From there he is taken by lorry, together with three other men, and shot in the olive-groves which cover the slopes above the road to the village of Alfacar. In 1940 the authorities in Granada attempted to conceal the assassination by declaring that Lorca had died 'in the month of August 1936 from war wounds'.

Plot

Act One

The curtain rises on an inner room in Bernarda's house, distinguished by its thick white walls. The room is empty and the silence oppressive in th—e heat of summer. The monotonous tolling of bells is the only sound to be heard.

The Servant enters, followed by Poncia, who has worked in Bernarda's house for thirty years. Her opening conversation with the Servant reveals that she has been attending the church service in honour of Bernarda's recently deceased husband, Antonio María Benavides, and, while her mistress is still at the service, Poncia has returned to the house to steal her food. As she eats, her resentment of Bernarda's tyrannical domination of her household – of family and servants alike – is made very clear.

When Poncia returns to the church service, the Servant coldly dismisses a beggar woman who comes to the house looking for food, and then reveals that she has herself been sexually abused by Bernarda's husband. Her sense of triumph at his death becomes a feigned lamentation as she hears the family return from the church, but this is immediately stifled and the Servant herself dismissed when Bernarda enters, followed by her five daughters and the village women who have come to pay tribute to her husband. While Bernarda asserts her authority for all to see, the asides of the village women reveal their hatred of her. She then leads them in prayers for the dead man in a formalised ritual which echoes the earlier church service, after which the women leave.

Bernarda now asks for a fan but immediately rejects the brightly decorated one offered by Adela, the youngest daughter, as frivolous and inappropriate to the occasion. She informs her daughters that the period of mourning for their father will last for eight years, and that they can occupy themselves by embroidering their trousseaus. Magdalena, the second daughter, insists that she will never marry, but is silenced by Bernarda, who, when told that the eldest girl, Angustias, has been listening to the scandalous gossip of a group of men, strikes her with her stick before angrily dismissing all the girls.

After their departure, Poncia reveals to Bernarda that the subject of the men's gossip was Paca la Roseta, a village girl who, on the previous night, had accompanied a group of young men to the olive-grove. Scandalised by the story, Bernarda boasts that there is no man in the village or the surrounding area worthy of her daughters.

When Bernarda and Poncia leave and the girls return, Martirio reveals to Amelia her sense of despair and her fear of men. A few moments later, Magdalena enters and informs them that Angustias, the eldest daughter by Bernarda's first marriage and the richest of all of them, is to be married to a local young man, Pepe el Romano, fourteen years her junior. The news is greeted with disbelief by Adela, who powerfully voices her desire to be free of the confinement of the house.

When they all rush out in response to the information that Pepe el Romano is coming down the street, Bernarda enters with Poncia. In the ensuing conversation it is revealed that Antonio María Benavides has left a substantial amount of money to Angustias, his stepdaughter, and far less to his natural daughters. When Angustias appears, her face heavily made-up, Bernarda angrily attacks her immodesty and furiously wipes the make-up from her face, despite her plea to be allowed out. Attracted by the noise, Magdalena demonstrates her resentment of Angustias's inheritance but is swiftly silenced by her mother. Their attention is engaged by the entrance of Bernarda's half-crazed mother, María Josefa, who, with flowers in her hair and at her breast, demands to be allowed out in order to marry a handsome young man on the seashore. Bernarda commands that the old woman be locked away in her room.

Act Two

The scene is set in another inner room where Angustias, Martirio, Magdalena and Amelia are sewing, attended by Poncia. Their opening remarks reveal that Adela is lying on her bed, unwell, and also draw attention to the stifling heat of the previous night.

Amelia observes that Pepe el Romano left Angustias's window (the traditional location for courting) at half-past one in the morning and agrees with Poncia that she also heard someone leaving at about four.

The girls' curiosity about Pepe and Angustias reveals their inexperience about sexual matters and is followed by Poncia's earthy and comic account of her first meeting at her window with her own future husband. Adela's appearance exposes a growing tension between her and Martirio, and, when the other girls have gone off to see some lace, leads to another confrontation between Adela and Poncia. The old servant, aware of Adela's fascination with Pepe el Romano, advises her to set aside her desires and attempts to console her with the hope that, if Angustias were to die in childbirth, she might still be able to marry Pepe. Adela, however, responds angrily, rejecting Poncia's advice and asserting that no one can stop her. The confrontation is interrupted first by Angustias and then by the arrival of Amelia, Martirio and Magdalena, who excitedly discuss the lace they have just seen. The tension between Adela and Martirio, as well as the resentment of Angustias, is still, however, much in evidence, and is broken only by the arrival of the harvesters who are passing the house on their way to the fields.

Stimulated by Poncia's description of these strong and vigorous young men, and moved by their songs of love, Adela and Magdalena rush out to watch them from the window of Adela's bedroom, accompanied by Poncia. Left together, Martirio and Amelia discuss again the presence of someone in the stable-yard in the early hours of the morning, but are interrupted by the furious entrance of Angustias, demanding to know who has stolen the portrait of Pepe el Romano from under her pillow. The sound of raised voices attracts the attention of Bernarda who, having interrogated her daughters without success, orders Poncia to search their rooms. The search reveals the portrait between the sheets of Martirio's bed, upon which Bernarda strikes her with her stick, provoking further bitter accusations amongst the young women. Bernarda angrily dismisses them, vowing to assert her authority even more strongly.

Left with Poncia, Bernarda expresses her regret that she, a servant, should have witnessed private family matters, and when Poncia attempts to warn her that there is something serious

happening of which she is unaware, Bernarda cruelly reminds
Poncia of her infamous origins and of her position as a servant. In
response, Poncia informs her that Pepe el Romano has been seen
talking to Angustias at half-past four in the morning. Angustias's
denial of it leads to further dissension and to Bernarda asserting
her authority once more. At this point the Servant enters with
news of a disturbance in the street. When the other women leave,
Martirio and Adela confront each other, the former threatening to
expose Adela's affair with Pepe el Romano, Adela asserting that
he will be hers. Outside, a young unmarried girl who has given
birth and tried to dispose of the baby is being dragged through
the street by angry and outraged villagers. As Bernarda calls for
her death, Adela clutches her stomach.

Act Three

The scene is set in an inner courtyard where Bernarda and her
daughters are finishing their evening meal. Prudencia, a
neighbour, has called on her way to church, and reveals her own
family problems: her husband has quarrelled with his brothers
over an inheritance and refuses to forgive his daughter for her
disobedience, both attitudes which meet with Bernarda's approval.
Prudencia reveals too that she is slowly going blind, and that the
mockery of the local children, who are unsympathetic to her
plight, will soon prevent her from attending church, her only
consolation in life. Her conversation with Bernarda is twice
interrupted by the sound of the stallion kicking against the stable
walls, before, on Bernarda's orders, he is released into the stable-
yard. Before she leaves, Prudencia is shown Angustias's
engagement-ring and the furniture which Bernarda has bought for
her at considerable expense. Both draw ironic comments from
Adela in particular.

   After Prudencia's departure, Adela goes for a stroll in the yard
and is accompanied, despite her protests, by Amelia and Martirio.
In their absence, Bernarda urges Angustias to forgive Martirio the
theft of Pepe el Romano's portrait, if only to preserve the
appearance of family unity. In reply, Angustias reveals that Pepe
seems distant when he visits her, as if his thoughts are elsewhere.

Bernarda advises her not to question him nor to let him see she is upset, least of all after their marriage.

Adela, Amelia and Martirio return from their walk. They have seen the white stallion in the stable-yard and react both to it and the star-lit sky in different ways: Adela with wonder, Amelia with fear, Martirio with indifference. Bernarda informs them that it is time for bed and, in reply to Adela's enquiry, indicates that Pepe el Romano will not be visiting Angustias tonight.

Bernarda now taunts Poncia with the observation that there is no evidence of 'something serious happening', as the servant had previously hinted. Poncia is unwilling to be drawn on the matter but attempts to unsettle her mistress by referring to the unpredictability of things in general. When Bernarda has gone to bed, Poncia reveals to the Servant the full extent of her fears: Bernarda's pride blinds her to what is happening, and things have gone too far already. Not only is Adela obsessed by Pepe el Romano and resolved to have him for herself, but Martirio will do everything in her power to stop her.

As the two servants prepare to retire for the night, Adela enters in order, she claims, to quench her thirst. When she and the servants have left the room, María Josefa enters, carrying in her arms a lamb to which she sings a lullaby. She is quickly followed by Adela, who, without speaking, slips out through the door into the yard. Martirio now enters and María Josefa tells her she intends to escape and that Pepe el Romano will destroy all the young women in the household. When Martirio has persuaded the old woman to return to her room, she crosses to the door to the yard and calls Adela, who appears immediately, her hair dishevelled and straw on her petticoat. In the bitter argument which develops between them, Adela boasts of her relationship with Pepe and provokes Martirio to the point where she cries out that she loves him too. Their raised voices quickly bring Bernarda from her bed, and she, learning from Martirio that Adela has been with Pepe in the stable, rushes out in search of him. A shot is heard, and when Bernarda and Martirio return, the latter claims that Pepe is dead. By the time Martirio reveals that Pepe has not been killed but has escaped, Adela has run in anguish to another room where she locks the door. When the door is opened Poncia's gesture and words indicate very clearly that Adela has hanged herself. Bernarda at once commands that her body be cut down, that the story be given out that Adela died a virgin, and that a new period of mourning begin.

Commentary

Lorca and the theatre of his time

Lorca's dozen or so full-length plays, written during a relatively short period of sixteen years, reveal a great variety of influences, both Spanish and foreign. As far as European theatre in the first quarter of the twentieth century was concerned, there was a clear reaction against the Naturalist movement of the nineteenth century. Broadly this had been a scientific approach which emphasised heredity and environment as the key 'determining' factors in the lives of human beings; in the theatre, it led playwrights to attempt to recreate the here and now of everyday reality, with individuals and groups of people shown to be influenced less by their own desires and aspirations than by heredity and environment. Because it emphasised the similarities rather than the differences between people, Naturalism in the theatre created a levelling of the classes presented on stage, and, in addition, blurred both the distinctions between the 'high' and the 'low', the 'serious' and the 'comic', and those individual moments in a play which are 'dramatic' or 'undramatic'. The influence of Naturalism can be seen quite clearly in the plays of Anton Chekhov (1860–1904) and Henrik Ibsen (1828–1906), though both dramatists were, of course, responsive to other movements in the theatre.

Directly opposed to Naturalism, with its emphasis on the material world, was Symbolism, which was concerned with the transcendental, the greater reality which lies beyond the mundane world in which we live, and which had been anticipated in the nineteenth century in the theory and practice of, for instance, Richard Wagner. In his music drama Wagner had attempted to evoke through archetypal characters and by means of a theatrical technique which combined music, poetry, acting and stage design those eternal truths which lie beyond the visible world. As far as twentieth-century theatre is concerned, it was the Belgian dramatist Maurice Maeterlinck (1862–1949) who led the way. In

The Blue Bird, written in 1905, two children, Tyltyl and Mytyl, embark on a quest to find the Blue Bird which will cure the sick child of a neighbour, are guarded by Light but obstructed by Night, and the Blue Bird escapes. The characters are clearly not so much individuals set in a particular time and space, as would have been the case in Naturalist drama, but archetypal beings who embody the very essence of human aspiration, struggle and ultimate failure, the symbolic nature of the characters and the stage action underpinned by stage design and movement which is highly stylised. In European theatre as a whole the same movement away from Naturalism was to be found in the theory and practice of such significant stage designers and directors as Adolphe Appia, Edward Gordon Craig and Max Reinhardt, all of whom favoured symbolical representation and a close integration of the different elements of performance in order to stir the imagination of an audience.

The early years of the twentieth century were also marked by the development of other significant movements in the Arts, such as Cubism, Futurism, Dadaism, Expressionism, and later on, in the 1920s, Surrealism. In their different ways they are movements which represent both a rejection of hitherto accepted values and ideals, and an attempt to find new ways of looking at the world. Expressionism, dating from about 1910, was given an added impulse by the terrible atrocities of the 1914–18 war and was often concerned, therefore, with positive values such as the creation of an equal and just society and the rejection of the machine age in favour of a more simple society. In order to communicate its message Expressionist theatre, in the hands of dramatists such as Ernst Toller and Georg Kaiser, employed exaggeration and distortion in characterisation, language and staging.

Surrealism, associated in particular with the Paris Surrealist group of the 1920s but evident before that, was concerned in part with the unconscious mind, with the inner rather than the outer man, with the illogical and the irrational, and with the expression of feelings and emotions uncontrolled by reason. In the theatre in France, Guillaume Apollinaire and Jean Cocteau, in plays such as *The Breasts of Tiresias* and *Parade*, both performed in 1917, set out to undermine the Naturalist tradition in order to suggest both the importance of the unconscious mind and the truth that lies beneath the appearance of things. In consequence, the technique of the plays is the very opposite of Naturalistic, employing all manner of exaggeration and distortion to evoke a world in which logic plays no part.

In Spain itself Naturalism had its equivalent in writers such as Benito Pérez Galdós (1843–1920), who, apart from being Spain's greatest novelist of the nineteenth century, also wrote twenty-two plays, and Jacinto Benavente (1866–1954), who dominated the Spanish theatrical scene for so many years. Both Galdós and Benavente reacted against the inflated neo-Romantic style which had characterised the theatre there in the latter part of the nineteenth century, and both were concerned in their own plays with a greater realism in relation to characters, background and language. This said, the theatre of Benavente did not change or evolve very much during his long career. Having discovered a successful formula, he largely settled for it, and in his hands, as well as in the hands of a number of other successful and popular dramatists, Spanish theatre remained for many years rather stagnant and undemanding.

Of the dramatists who, influenced by cultural trends outside Spain, attempted to advance the cause of Spanish theatre through bold experiment, the most important figure before Lorca was undoubtedly Ramón del Valle-Inclán (1866–1936). His early work, in particular *The Savage Plays*, reveals the clear influence of European Symbolism, for it is concerned, in its portrayal of the history of Don Juan Manuel Montenegro and his family, with the evocation of timeless and universal issues, above all good and evil and the redemption of Man through suffering. Valle-Inclán's technique, moreover, is highly reminiscent in its synthesis of stage settings, constumes, movement, lighting and dialogue of the ideas on theatre of Symbolist stage designers and producers such as Adolphe Appia and Edward Gordon Craig.

By 1920, and partly in response to the horrors of the First World War, Valle-Inclán's Symbolist phase had given way to his theory and practice of the grotesque, *esperpentismo*, an approach to dramatic writing which is defined in *Bohemian Lights*, written in 1920, which owes something to Expressionism as well as to the puppet tradition, and which Valle-Inclán believed more appropriate to the expression of the absurd and grotesque nature of Spanish life as he saw it. Other significant writers of the time who turned their back on Naturalism were Miguel de Unamuno

(1864–1936), whose stark, unadorned plays often exteriorise emotional and intellectual conflicts, and Jacinto Grau (1877–1958), whose work after 1918 expresses the preoccupations of that time in a style which closely integrates the different elements of stage performance.

As far as Spain is concerned, mention must be made too of the important centuries-old tradition of puppet theatre and farce. Cervantes, for example, had introduced a puppet show, *Master Peter's Puppet Show*, into the second part of *Don Quixote*, published in 1615, while the same year also saw the appearance of a collection of eight short plays, *Interludes*, which in their presentation of ingenious situations and boldly comic characters were models of their kind. Valle-Inclán in his grotesque plays, Jacinto Grau in *Mr Pygmalion*, written in 1921, and Carlos Arniches (1866–1943) in his *grotesque farces*, continued that tradition in the first two decades or so of the twentieth century.

Lorca's first play, *The Butterfly's Evil Spell*, reveals the very clear influence of Symbolism, as well as, in all probability, the direct influence of Maeterlinck's *The Blue Bird*. Through the story of Curianito, the young cockroach who falls in love with the Butterfly but is rejected by her, Lorca explores the themes of love, frustration and death which are so central to his own existence. This, moreover, is enhanced by Lorca's highly stylised presentation of the characters and events which transforms the particularity of the on-stage action into a visual metaphor with which we can all identify. There are strong elements of Symbolism too in Lorca's second play, *Mariana Pineda*, despite the fact that the subject is historical and, to that extent, more 'realistic'. Once more the themes are the characteristic Lorca themes of passion and frustration, but, as well as this, the purity of Mariana herself is set against the evil of Pedrosa, the Chief of Police, while the conflict between them, itself universal in its implications, is set within an essentially poetic and symbolic frame created by the white of walls and costume, the black of Pedrosa's clothes, and the approach of night. The concerns of Symbolism, including concepts of staging which are strictly anti-Naturalistic, are to be found throughout Lorca's theatre.

At the same time, his interest in puppet theatre was evident from an early stage. In 1922, two years after the disastrous opening of *The Butterfly's Evil Spell*, he completed a play for puppets, *The Tragicomedy of Don Cristóbal and Señorita Rosita*, and in the following year organised a puppet show in Granada with Manuel de Falla. It was an aspect of his work which was, in conjunction with farce, to become more important in the years ahead, for between 1924 and 1935 *The Shoemaker's Wonderful Wife*, *The Love of Don Perlimplín for Belisa in his Garden*, and *The Puppet Play of Don Cristóbal* were all written and performed.

Lorca's interest in this tradition and his championing of it in his own work is easily explained, for, like Symbolism, puppet-theatre and farce are anti-Naturalistic, characterised by a simplicity and a boldness which allowed Lorca that freedom of expression, that spontaneity and vitality which he believed to be the essential ingredients of a living theatre. So, in the prologue to *The Puppet Play of Don Cristóbal* he refers to 'the delicious and hard language of the puppets', and later the director of the play itself wishes to 'fill the theatre with fresh wheat', a clear pointer to the stale Naturalism of much contemporary Spanish theatre. Although the characters of *The Shoemaker's Wonderful Wife* are played by actors, the technique is very much that of the puppet play as they engage in vigorous physical and verbal action against settings which in their boldness echo the liveliness of the characters. They are features of Lorca's theatrical style which, in varying degrees, are to be seen in all his plays.

Surrealism came into its own in Lorca's work in the theatre in two major plays, *The Public* and *When Five Years Pass*, completed in 1930 and 1931 respectively, though its influence is evident both before and after these particular plays. Lorca's friendships with Luis Buñuel and Salvador Dalí proved crucial to the dramatist's familiarity with 'avant-garde' movements in European culture, as well as to his exposure to the theories of Sigmund Freud, much read at the Residencia de Estudiantes in the 1920s. There are clear Surrealist elements in the short piece, *Buster Keaton's Spin*, written in 1925, but it was the emotional crisis of 1929 which led Lorca to express his true inner anguish in the two full-length and enormously ambitious plays mentioned above. In both *The Public*, his only overtly gay play, and *When Five Years Pass*, arguably his most accomplished and striking piece of theatre, Lorca's personal obsessions – love, frustration, passing time and death – are expressed through an action which is essentially dreamlike, in which the characters are seen to be echoes of or contrasts to each

other and in which their unconscious fears frequently assume
frightening external forms. Thus, at a crucial moment in Act One
of *When Five Years Pass*, the on-stage characters of the Young Man,
the Old Man, the Friend and the Second Friend are suddenly
confronted by a nightmarish scene involving the Dead Child and
the Dead Cat which exteriorises the deep-seated anxieties of all
the onlookers. Greatly influenced by Surrealism, both plays also
reveal in their strongly visual character and in their fluid
movement the imprint of Symbolism, Expressionism, puppet-
theatre and cinema. Once more Lorca shows himself to be
constantly seeking new forms of expression, a fundamental aspect
of his work which is also evident in his screenplay of 1929, *Trip to
the Moon*.

These various influences come together as well, of course, in
Lorca's great plays of the 1930s, including the so-called 'rural
trilogy' of *Blood Wedding, Yerma*, and *The House of Bernarda Alba*. In
one sense plays whose subjects, characters and settings are located
in the Spanish countryside suggest Naturalism rather than any
kind of stylisation, but the opposite is in fact true, despite the fact
that *Blood Wedding* and *The House of Bernarda Alba* have their origins
in real-life events. In the first place, the names which Lorca gives
his characters have, for the most part, a generic and archetypal
quality: in *Blood Wedding* the Mother, the Father, the Bridegroom,
the Bride, the Wife, the Neighbour; in *Yerma* the Old Woman, the
First Girl, the Second Girl. Even when there are real names they
often have a symbolic resonance: in *Blood Wedding* the two halves
of Leonardo's name suggest a 'burning lion'; and in *The House of
Bernarda Alba*, the surname Alba has associations with 'dawn' and
therefore 'brightness' and 'light', while the connections of
Angustias with anguish and Martirio with martyrdom are evident
enough. In addition, Lorca's constant linking of the characters of
these plays to the soil, the trees, the heat, water, the seasons, in
short to the world of Nature, creates a very strong sense of their
universality. In the final acts of *Blood Wedding* and *Yerma*,
moreover, the effect is enhanced and a sense of timelessness
created by the appearance of non-human figures: in the former
Moon and Death (the Beggar-Woman); in the latter the fertility
figures of Male and Female. Lorca's use of poetry in both plays,
and especially in *Blood Wedding*, also has the effect of universalising
the particular through suggestive metaphor, while his suggestions

for staging – stark, stylised settings, dramatic lighting effects, and bold movement, including dance – reveal an intention at the opposite extreme from Naturalism. And even if, in *The House of Bernarda Alba*, the poetry of the other two plays is pared away and there seems to be a greater realism, a closer examination suggests that Lorca's predilection is still for an overall stylisation. Indeed, in their different ways the three plays of the rural trilogy can be seen to combine elements of Symbolism, Expressionism, Surrealism – consider the forest scene of *Blood Wedding* – as well as the puppet tradition, all fused into an anti-Naturalistic style of which he increasingly proved to be a master.

The real-life source of *The House of Bernarda Alba*

Like *Blood Wedding*, *The House of Bernarda Alba* is firmly grounded in reality. In 1907 the Lorca family had moved from the village of Fuente Vaqueros, some ten miles from Granada, to a neighbouring village called Asquerosa, where they owned a substantial house. Although they subsequently moved to Granada itself, they continued to return to the house in Asquerosa (later called Valderrubio) for a few months every summer. In later life Lorca observed to his friend, the Chilean diplomat, Carlos Morla Lynch:

'There is, not very far from Granada, a small village where my parents owned a small property: Valderrubio. In the house adjoining ours lived "Doña Bernarda", a very old widow who kept an inexorable and tyrannical watch over her unmarried daughters. They were prisoners deprived of all free will, so I never spoke with them; but I saw them pass like shadows, always silent and always dressed in black ... ; at the edge of the yard there was a shared well, with no water, and I used to go down into it to watch that strange family whose enigmatic behaviour fascinated me. And I observed them. It was a silent and cold hell in the African sun, a tomb for the living under the harsh rule of a dark jailer. And so was born ... *The House of Bernarda Alba* ...'

The 'Doña Bernarda' of Lorca's account, which had become somewhat embroidered with the passage of time, was in fact

Frasquita Alba Sierra, who would have been about fifty years of age in 1907. The house in which she lived was not, however, 'adjoining ours' but next door to the house occupied by Lorca's Aunt Mathilde and her family. The shared well lay at the back of these two houses, and conversations on one side of their dividing wall could be heard, via the well, on the other. Frasquita Alba, though, was not a widow during Lorca's childhood, nor does she seem to have had a reputation for the kind of tyranny displayed by Bernarda Alba towards her children.

Frasquita Alba had seven children, five daughters and two sons, of which two were named Amelia and Magdalena. Lorca retained these names for two of his characters and gave the name of another daughter, Prudencia, to the neighbour who visits Bernarda in Act Three. Frasquita's daughter, Amelia, was married to José Benavides, who was known as Pepico el de Roma because he came from the village of Romilla or Roma la Chica. He was therefore the source for Lorca's Pepe el Romano, though in the play the name Benavides became the surname of Bernarda's husband, Antonio María Benavides. Similarly, other characters who appear or are mentioned in the play had a basis in reality. Bernarda's half-mad mother, María Josefa, was based on a Lorca relative who suffered from erotic hallucinations. Poncia, a key figure in the play, was modelled on a real servant, though not one who worked for Frasquita Alba. And both Enrique Humanes, who in the play is said to be interested in Martirio, and Maximiliano, whose wife is taken to the olive-grove by a group of men, were based on real people. In short, it is true to say that of the characters who appear in the play in either major or minor roles, most have a solid grounding in reality.

If the characters are rooted in the real world, so is the house in which Bernarda and her family live. From the outset we have a clear impression of its thick walls. In Act One we can visualise the yard (the *patio*), where the men are provided with drinks, the stable-yard (the *corral*) beyond it, and the great door (the *portón*) to the street at the end of the yard, through which Angustias eavesdrops on the men outside. All the bedrooms are on the ground floor (the upper floor was used for storage), some of them at the front and side of the house, facing the street. Such is Adela's room from which, in Act One, she can see Pepe el Romano when he turns the corner, and where, according to

Poncia in Act Two, she was standing 'almost naked' when Pepe came to court Angustias. The latter's bedroom too faces the street, and from there she speaks to her suitor through its barred window. In Act Three the yard, the stable-yard and the stables themselves become the focal points of the action. From the stables, beyond the stable-yard, the stallion is heard kicking against the walls. From there it is released into the stable-yard where Adela, Amelia and Martirio observe it when they take a breath of fresh air. Later Adela sneaks out into the stable-yard in order to meet Pepe el Romano in the stables. Lorca creates a very strong sense, therefore, of the geography of the house and of the movements of the characters within its different locations. It seems likely, though, that the house of Bernarda Alba is not based on Frasquita Alba's house, which Lorca never entered, but on the Lorca house around the corner from it in Calle Iglesias.

Very real too is the play's evocation of a community and its traditional way of life. The arrival of the mourners in Act One, the distribution of the lemonade, and the ritualistic chanting which follows, are typical of life in the villages of Spain. If Bernarda's eight years of mourning seem excessive, long periods of mourning were certainly a feature of Spanish rural life. So too was the division between men and women, the latter's purely domestic role exemplified in the sewing and embroidery of Bernarda's daughters. In this context the prospect of inevitable spinsterhood, or of an arranged and loveless marriage, was very much a fact of life, as was Poncia's assessment in Act Two of the comparative freedom of men: '. . . two weeks after the wedding a man leaves the bed for the table, and then the table for the tavern. And the woman who doesn't accept it wastes away crying in a corner'. The greater freedom of men is suggested by the behaviour of the harvesters in Act Two, and their arrival in the village also suggests an annual event. Equally authentic are the gossip and criticism alluded to throughout the play and which are so ingrained in tight-knit communities; the quarrels over land and inheritance, as frequent now as they were then; and the scandal and high emotion created by illegitimacy, exemplified in the villagers' treatment of the young girl at the end of Act Two.

In short, Lorca constructs in *The House of Bernarda Alba* a house, a group of characters and a community, all of which have a strong sense of realism. Indeed, when he was writing the play, he

would finish a scene and cry out excitedly: 'There's not a drop of
poetry! Reality! Pure realism!' He also wrote on the title-page:
'The poet points out that these three acts are intended to be a
photographic documentary', in other words a true record of village
life. He wanted, of course, to emphasise the difference in terms of
realism between his latest play and earlier plays like *Blood Wedding*
and *Doña Rosita the Spinster*, in which poetic elements were so
prominent.

The social background and meaning of the play

There can be no doubt that the realism of *The House of Bernarda
Alba* was firmly linked to Lorca's intention, announced in the
newspaper *El Sol* in 1934, of writing 'modern plays on the age we
live in', in which he would expose the ills, social and moral, of
the Spain of his time. In this respect *Play Without a Title*, on which
he began work in 1935 and of which only one act remains, is his
most overtly political play, for it not only presents the bitter
conflict between Left and Right which led to the Spanish Civil
War one year later, but also attacks the Right for its indifference
towards the suffering of the poor and the less fortunate. In *The
House of Bernarda Alba* the political element is less obvious, but
Lorca's reference to it as a 'photographic documentary', as well as
his choice of a sub-title – 'A Drama of Women in the Villages of
Spain' – makes it very clear indeed that the play is intended, on
one level at least, to be a commentary on particular aspects of
contemporary Spanish life.

   In the character of Bernarda herself, Lorca embodied many of
the attitudes of the Spain of his time of which he disapproved.
She owns a substantial house, has people working for her on her
land, and is wealthy enough to buy fine lace and expensive
furniture for Angustias's marriage. In short, money gives her
power over others, and a sense of social superiority which leads
her to regard those less fortunate than herself with scorn – 'The
poor are like animals' (Act One) – and to treat those in her
employment with such scant regard that her servants are driven to
steal her food when the opportunity arises. Gerald Brenan has
noted that in 1930 on the large Andalusian estates, from which
the owners were usually absent, landless labourers were paid the

miserable sum of 3 to 3·5 pesetas for an eight-hour day for four to
five months of the year, and in summer, in terrible heat, 4 to 6
pesetas for a twelve-hour day, while on remote farms the figure
fell to 2·25 pesetas for men and 1 to 1·25 for women (*The Spanish
Labyrinth*, 1943, pp. 114–26). Bernarda is not, of course, the owner
of a large estate, but her callousness is similar to that which Lorca
had himself encountered in many of the landowners in the region
around Fuente Vaqueros and Asquerosa, and which he, as a
socialist, came to detest.

Bernarda is also the firm advocate of strongly traditional
attitudes, amongst which the subservience of women to men, as
well as their entirely domestic role, are much to the fore. In
Hispanic countries in general women have for centuries been
repressed by men, a discrimination which in Spain was
accentuated not only by the teachings of the Catholic Church but
also by the country's historical and cultural contact with Islam
over a long period of time. The duty of the married woman,
therefore, was that of wife and mother, attending to her husband's
needs, running the home, and producing children. As for single
women, as her own daughters prove, life must be devoted to
sewing and embroidery. Bernarda's statement in Act One reflects
that view – 'A needle and thread for women. A whip and a mule
for men' – as does her advice to Angustias in Act Three about
obedience to her husband-to-be – 'Speak if he speaks and look at
him when he looks at you'. In the early years of the Second
Spanish Republic (1931–6), which Lorca strongly supported,
attempts to improve the status of women were made by the left-
wing government but were undermined by the Right when they
returned to power in 1933. Bernarda exemplifies the views of the
Right and would therefore have applauded the Francoist view of
'a woman's place is in the home' which would dominate Spanish
life for almost forty years after the triumph of the Right in the
Civil War.

In sexual matters Bernarda also speaks for a narrow-minded
society which, indoctrinated by the Church, saw the sexual act as
intended only for procreation and neatly divided women into
either saints or whores. In this context the behaviour of Paca la
Roseta, who in Act One is described by Poncia as having
entertained a group of men in the olive-grove, is condemned out
of hand – 'She's the only loose woman in the village' – and, at

the end of Act Two, Bernarda's attitude towards the unmarried girl who has borne a child is that of a total bigot devoid of any understanding and compassion: 'A red-hot coal in the place of her sin!' In contrast, her acceptance of the sexual excesses of men, for whom the experience of pre- and post-marital sex was merely a sign of their manliness or 'machismo', is equally rooted in tradition, an attitude which in itself denies the possibility of movement towards sexual equality.

Sexual behaviour is closely connected with another area in which Bernarda's views are entirely traditional: the concept of family honour, name and reputation, so deeply ingrained in the Spanish temperament. For centuries a male-dominated society had been obsessed with a notion of self-esteem which has little to do with what one is but everything to do with how one is perceived by others. That perception may clearly be influenced for the worse by, amongst other things, sexual misdemeanours which become the subject of public gossip, thereby tarnishing the family name. Bernarda is therefore always anxious that her daughters should not give rise to such gossip, and for this reason, at the end of Act Three, she insists that the villagers be informed that Adela died a virgin. In this context it is worth recalling that the Penal Code of 1870, which allowed a husband to 'cleanse his honour with blood' if his wife were found committing adultery or if his wife or daughter were raped, was not dispensed with until 1963. Although that precise situation does not exist in Lorca's play, Bernarda shares that fanatical mentality. On a different level her concern with good name leads to her criticism of the Servant in Act One – 'You should have made sure that this was cleaner for the mourners' – and to her insistence in Act Two that her daughters should not be heard arguing: 'The neighbours will have their ears glued to the walls'. It is, of course, an obsession with such things which underlies Bernarda's hypocrisy, as well as her cruelty and lack of compassion, characteristics which Lorca had himself encountered in the highly traditional, conservative and narrow-minded society of his day, and of which in the end he was a victim.

Inasmuch as Bernarda's views are those of her time, they are shared by other inhabitants of her household and of her village. Though different from her mistress in many ways, Poncia is very like her both in her acceptance of the traditional roles of men and

women and in her concern with reputation: 'I want to live in a
respectable house. I don't want to be disgraced in my old age!'
Similarly, even though they resent it, Bernarda's daughters
acknowledge and mostly accept the freedom enjoyed by men, as
well as their own domestic role, and they recognise too how
gossip and criticism damage the family name. Of the people
outside the household, Prudencia reveals that her husband's
quarrel with his brothers over an inheritance has become the
subject of common gossip and therefore the source of his damaged
reputation and of considerable family anguish. Clearly, what is
true of Bernarda and her daughters in terms of traditional
attitudes is also true of other households and families not only in
her own village but in towns and villages throughout Spain. Given
the 'realism' of the play, there can be no doubt that Lorca was
concerned with presenting to a contemporary Spanish audience
the reality of Spanish provincial life – indeed, of much of Spanish
life in general – as he perceived it. In no other Lorca play is the
sense of contemporary Spanish life quite so strong.

The broader meaning: symbolism and imagery

Although the realistic level and the social implications of *The House
of Bernarda Alba* are of great importance, the play would not
possess such a lasting and world-wide appeal if it did not also
have a level of meaning which extends beyond the local and the
particular. This said, it is important to understand that the
broader meaning of Lorca's work as a whole stems ultimately
from his creation of a solid, credible world firmly rooted in reality.
But his dramatic method is distinguished less by simple realism
than by a realism which is frequently symbolic.

On one level the play's three stage settings suggest real
locations: the inner room of Act One with its thick, white walls,
its arched doorways and rush-bottomed chairs; the second inner
room of Act Two, again with white walls, chairs and doors
leading off to the bedrooms; and the inner courtyard of Act Three
where the family eat, the sound of plates and silverware can be
heard, and light comes from inside the house. On the other hand,
the elements which compose the stage-pictures are highly selective
and quickly acquire a symbolic resonance. The whiteness of the

walls, which links all three settings, points to both the virginity of
Bernarda's daughters and the monotonous, unchanging routine of
their lives, the latter reinforced by the sameness of the arched
doorways and the tolling bells. In addition, the oppressive silence
weighs heavily, suggesting the way in which the young women are
themselves burdened by the nature of their existence. Even before
the characters appear, Lorca creates a powerful image of
imprisonment and oppression. Furthermore, the physical character
of Bernarda's house evokes other houses in her village and beyond
it, and by so doing extends to them similar associations. Not
without cause did Lorca describe his play as 'A Drama of Women
in the Villages of Spain'.

As far as the characters' names are concerned, they are in one
sense more realistic than the names which Lorca gave his
characters in *Blood Wedding* – the Bride, the Bridegroom, the
Mother, etc. – for they are typical of the names to be found in
the kind of society represented in the play. On the other hand,
some of them are immediately suggestive of emotional and
spiritual states – Martirio (martyrdom and suffering) and Angustias
(anguish) in particular – while the characters themselves are, in
appearance and manner, archetypal. Bernarda, dressed in black
throughout the play, is the very personification of a narrow-
mindedness which stifles any kind of joy, while the colour of her
clothes is itself also suggestive of the growing Fascism which
affected Europe in the 1930s. Her daughters too, similarly dressed,
reflect the inescapable darkness of their own futures under their
mother's roof, with the exception of Adela, the epitome of youth
and vitality, and thus of opposition to the strictures placed upon
her life. It is significant, of course, that at the very moment when,
in Act One, she voices her refusal to be confined in the house –
'No, I shan't get used to it! I don't want to be shut away!' – she
should be wearing her green dress, a colour which immediately
links her with the vitality and fertility of Nature itself. Indeed,
through the characters of the play and the images associated with
them, Lorca evokes two entirely different worlds: the vibrant world
of instinct and passion on the one hand; the represssive world of
social convention and tradition on the other. The conflict between
them, embodied in the particular action and characters of the
play, becomes therefore, as it does in *Blood Wedding* and *Yerma*, the
expression of a fundamental and universal conflict between those

life-enhancing and life-denying forces which have been at the heart of human experience from time immemorial.

The black of Bernarda's dress, almost unrelieved throughout the play, has powerful echoes elsewhere. The house itself is in semi-darkness, its windows shuttered so that the sunlight barely penetrates. In every way this is a world of half-light. By Act Three, moreover, the action is increasingly enveloped in the blackness of night which, in turn, reflects the emotional darkness in which many of the characters are hopelessly lost. As far as Adela is concerned, her suicide plunges her into eternal darkness, and condemns her sisters to a further period of mourning and confinement to the house, to the darkness of increasing despair, and perhaps – in Martirio's case – to the shadowy world of madness reflected in the grandmother.

Linked to the notion of darkness is that of enclosure and imprisonment. The thick walls described in the opening stage-direction initiate a prison image which is subsequently developed in other ways. During the visit of the mourners in Act One, María Josefa is locked away, and when she escapes from her room at the end of the act, Bernarda commands once more: 'Lock her up!' In the same act Magdalena refers to 'this dark room' in which she and her sisters spend their days, while Bernarda describes the imminent eight years of mourning as if 'we'd sealed the doors and the windows'. In Act Two the notion of enclosure is reinforced by Poncia's reference to the house as a convent – 'It's been my lot to serve in this convent' – as well as by the fact that the courtship of Angustias and Pepe el Romano takes place at the window with its iron bars (the traditional *reja*). In the same act Bernarda describes herself as jailer to her daughters – 'five chains – for each of you' – an image reinforced in Act Three when Adela seizes and breaks her mother's stick – 'You aren't my jailer any more!' After Adela's death, Bernarda's emphasis on mourning and silence anticipates an even greater confinement than before.

The themes of death and lifelessness are strongly emphasised throughout the play. In Act Two, for example, Angustias refers to the importance of her own wealth – 'Besides, gold in the coffers is worth more than dark eyes in a pretty face' – in a way in which her mother, one of the richest people in the region, has doubtless done on many occasions. But the yellow of gold, in contrast to other allusions to yellow in the course of the play, can be seen to have a decidedly negative meaning: Bernarda's exploitation of her workers in the interests of profit; the envy and resentment which Angustias's inheritance provokes amongst her sisters; and the quarrel between Prudencia's husband and his brothers over money bequeathed to them. In short, gold and gold coins are associated with feelings and relationships which are far from positive. Equally, Bernarda's reference in Act One to 'this terrible village without a river' is also extremely suggestive, for it evokes a picture not only of a sun-baked river-bed but of people who, emotionally and spiritually, are lacking in any vital or creative spirit.

In contrast, a network of images and allusions points to the vibrant and positive world of natural instinct and passion to which Adela is linked by the green of her dress. The olive-grove, largely green in colour and a recurring symbol in Lorca's work for the vitality and fertility of Nature, is the setting for the love-making of Paca la Roseta and the young men who take her there. In Act Two Poncia describes one of the strong young harvesters as having 'green eyes', while in Act One Adela's fan, which Bernarda angrily rejects, is decorated with green and red flowers. Red is, of course, the traditional colour of passion, and in the text of the play again helps to evoke a world completely different from that of Bernarda. When, for example, the harvesters pass the house in Act Two, their song refers to roses in an unmistakably sexual manner:

> Open your doors and windows,
> You girls who live in the town.
> The reaper wants your roses
> To decorate his crown.

In addition, if the white of the walls, as well as the white of the sheets which the women sew in Act Two, points to the endless monotony of their lives and their domestic tasks, it also evokes in Adela's case the flawless beauty of her flesh, so attractive to Pepe el Romano. Again, when in Act Three María Josefa refers to foam – 'and we shall be foam. Why is there no foam here?' – the image of the sea suggests creativity, water which is the source of life, and contrasts with the black of mourning which dominates Bernarda's house and the dry river-bed which characterises the village. As well as this, María Josefa's dream of marrying a young man 'on the seashore' conjures up a picture of open spaces and freedom which are entirely absent from Bernarda's house. Yellow too is used to evoke a world of beauty and vitality: the young and vigorous harvesters are described in Act Two as reaping 'in tongues of fire', and are linked therefore to the life-giving and enhancing power of sunlight, while the cornfields in which they work are witness to the creativity of Nature herself. In short, Lorca uses imagery and symbol instinctively and suggestively in order to evoke through particular actions, locations and characters their broader and more universal meanings. The greatness of *The House of Bernarda Alba* lies not in Lorca's creation on stage of a particular family in a particular house, but in the way he is able to transform that slice of Spanish life into a kind of mirror in which, in varying degrees, we can all see our own experience reflected.

The characters

Bernarda Alba
Bernarda Alba is one of the great parts in twentieth-century drama, a dominant figure whose presence is felt even when she is not on stage. Our initial impression of her is formed from the conversation of Poncia and the Servant – 'Bossy, domineering creature!', 'Tyrant of all she surveys' – and is quickly confirmed by her first dramatic entrance and her imperious command to the latter: 'Silence!' Between this and her final identical instruction to her weeping daughters, she dominates both them and her servants verbally and physically, striking her daughters with her stick and displaying a cruelty which even her old servants find worthy of comment. Her behaviour stems in part from her economic power, which allows her to exploit her workers and to enjoy prestige in the community, yet it also has to do, paradoxically, with her sense of vulnerability. This is linked, clearly, to the villagers' eagerness to pounce on any scandal in order to blacken Bernarda's name, and in this context to the ever-present possibility of sexual misdemeanours on the part of her daughters. It is ironic, therefore, that she should prove so blind to what is happening under her very nose, though, as with her angry rejection of

Poncia's attempts to alert her, her blindness is the inevitable consequence of her pride and her sense of infallibility. To that extent Bernarda helps unwittingly to bring about the very situation she seeks to avoid, which in turn allows us to feel for her a degree of pity we might not expect to feel for such a harsh and uncompromising character.

A particularly interesting, if unstated, aspect of the play concerns Bernarda's relationship with Angustias. Her physical attack on Angustias in Act One, when she wipes the powder from her face, is said to stem from her outrage that Angustias should put on make-up on the day of her father's funeral, but it occurs, significantly, after the revelation that Bernarda's husband, who is Angustias's stepfather, has left in his will much more money to her than to his four natural daughters. Could it be, then, that Antonio María Benavides, who has sexually taken advantage of the Servant, has favoured Angustias financially because of some closer relationship with her? And does Bernarda suspect it? This is a household and a community in which much is hidden and many secrets are cloaked in silence.

Angustias

At thirty-nine Angustias is the oldest of Bernarda's five girls and the only daughter of her first marriage. She is described by Poncia in Act Two as ageing rapidly, being narrow-waisted and having delicate health, while her sisters refer rather scathingly to her thinness and to the fact that, like her father, she 'talks through her nose'. Any existing lack of warmth towards her because she is only their half-sister is exacerbated in the play by other things, in particular by her arranged marriage to Pepe el Romano and the large inheritance from her stepfather. Well aware of her sisters' resentment and envy, Angustias reacts by flaunting both her wealth and her forthcoming marriage in a way which is probably uncharacteristically spirited, for she is certainly inexperienced and timid in matters of love and, alone with her mother, reveals herself to be extremely uncertain about what lies ahead: 'I ought to be happy but I'm not'. She is, at bottom, a rather sad figure who finds herself in a situation she cannot cope with.

Magdalena

Nine years younger than Angustias, Magdalena is Bernarda's eldest daughter by her second marriage and, it would seem, her father's favourite: 'The only one her father loved'. This being the case, her expectations of inheritance are natural but in the event thwarted, and lie therefore at the heart of much of her bitterness towards Angustias in the course of the play. In addition, the latter's proposed marriage deepens Magdalena's existing pessimism, already evident in Act One – 'I know I'll never get married' – and fans even more her resentment of her sister, forcing her to state in Act Two that she will not sew a stitch for any children Angustias might have. At other times there are signs of a much more caring nature, for she makes the green dress for Adela and wishes only for her happiness, but even in this context her bitterness towards Angustias can make her cut Adela to the quick, as in Act One: 'The best thing she can do is give it [the dress] to Angustias for her wedding to Pepe el Romano!' In important respects Magdalena is also like her mother, echoing her views on class – 'Each class does what it must' – and the role of women. After thirty years she has accepted the inevitable and unchanging nature of things.

Amelia

Twenty-seven years old, Amelia is neither as disillusioned as Magdalena, nor as tormented as Martirio, nor as assertive as Adela. In matters of love she is inexperienced and naive, as her reactions to the courtship of Angustias and the sexual activities of the harvesters suggest: 'I get so embarrassed by that sort of thing!' Such naivety is also accompanied by a more general timidity in relation to anything strange or potentially dangerous, as in the appearance of the white stallion in Act Three – 'It was frightening. He was like a ghost'. At other times she can be more spirited, refusing, like Magdalena, to look after Angustias's future children, and mocking the latter's accusation that she or one of her sisters has stolen Pepe's picture: 'It's not as if Pepe were a silver Saint Bartholomew!' It is perhaps surprising, given her rather passive nature, that Amelia should be so close to Martirio – 'always together, like two little sheep' – but that closeness could well be explained by the fact that they are so different.

Martirio

Twenty-four and the second youngest of the five daughters, Martirio is one of the play's most interesting characters. Her physical unattractiveness – in Act Two Adela scathingly alludes to her hump back – accounts both for her depression and for her attitude to men: 'God has made me weak and ugly and kept them away from me for ever'. On the other hand, Martirio's sexual feelings are strong and her sense of frustration intense, which therefore exacerbates her jealousy towards Angustias, promised to Pepe el Romano, and Adela, secretly involved with him. The proximity of her room to Adela's means that Martirio watches her every move – 'She follows me everywhere . . . She doesn't let me breathe' – which transforms envy and jealousy into a hatred whose full extent is revealed at the end of Act Two: 'I saw how he embraced you! . . . I'll see you dead first!' Poncia's description of her as a 'well of poison' is truly accurate, and yet her dramatic revelation in Act Three that she too loves Pepe el Romano – 'Yes! Why should I hide my head in shame?' – invites an unexpected pity for a woman who, for all her unattractiveness, feels passionately but in vain. Here is someone who has none of Adela's qualities but who, like her, cannot control her feelings: 'My heart is full of an evil force. In spite of myself, it's drowning me.' In Martirio, Lorca has created a character, we feel, whom he truly understands.

Adela

At twenty years of age, Adela is the youngest and the most attractive of Bernarda's daughters. On the one hand, her youth accounts for her spirited and spontaneous reaction to things, such as Magdalena's reminder in Act One of the period of mourning imposed by their mother: 'No, I shan't get used to it! I don't want to be shut away!' On the other hand, her youth also explains her naive and increasingly headstrong behaviour, notably in relation to Pepe el Romano. Given the fact that her attraction to him is nothing new, her rejection in Act Two of Poncia's sensible advice that patience is the best policy bears all the hallmarks of impulsive and defiant youth: 'I'd leap right over you. You're only a servant. And I'd leap over my mother too'. At the same time, Adela becomes more cunning and more devious as the action develops.

When, for instance, Martirio is discovered to have stolen Pepe's picture, Adela seizes the opportunity to fix the blame on her precisely to remove from herself any suspicion of her interest in him: 'It wasn't a joke. You've never liked jokes! It was something else that was boiling inside . . .'

It is also very much in character that the revelation of her illicit affair with Pepe el Romano should provoke in her not regret but defiance and triumph, a naive but understandable sense of exultation that she has experienced something which her sisters have not. It is a sense of power which is as reckless as it is irrational, and in the final moments of the play Adela's initial spontaneity is quickly transformed into a total lack of control, triumph into despair, and this, in turn, into self-destruction. Adela's tragedy is that her longing for life, which so distinguishes her from her sisters, should finally deprive her of it.

María Josefa

Sixty years older than Adela, María Josefa is in certain respects the closest to her in terms of her instincts and desires. Afflicted by senile dementia, she reveals that mixture of irrationality and lucidity which characterises many old people. Thus, while her dream of marrying a young man on the seashore is pure fantasy, her observation that all her grand-daughters long for Pepe el Romano and that he will destroy them is extremely perceptive, as is her description of Bernarda's predatory nature: 'Bernarda, leopard face'. The way in which she drifts between fantasy and reality, and the expression of youthful dreams in a mind and body ravaged by time, make her a figure of great pathos, not unlike King Lear in the second half of Shakespeare's play.

Poncia

Poncia, like Bernarda, is sixty years old, typical of her class in her practicality and her earthiness, yet striking too in her individuality. Her uninhibited enjoyment of life is evident on several occasions: her delight in the priest's chanting; her account of Paca la Roseta's sexual exploits; and her description of her husband-to-be's first visit to her window many years ago: 'Then Evaristo came closer and closer, as if he wanted to squeeze through the bars, and he said very quietly: "Come here, let me feel you!" ' At the same time, sexual pleasures in particular are for her, a sixty-year-old widow, to be savoured at second hand, and beneath her laughter there is, perhaps, a sense of regret at things now past.

Poncia's common sense, the product both of her background and of her experience, is much in evidence, as when in Act Two she offers Bernarda's daughters advice about men and marriage, and later recommends Adela to be patient in the matter of Pepe el Romano: 'Your sister Angustias is delicate. She won't survive the first birth . . .' It is, however, in her relationship with Bernarda that Poncia's experience serves her best. Having worked in the house for thirty years, Poncia knows Bernarda's strengths and weaknesses, and, if she is abused and exploited by her, proves expert at exploiting her in turn, employing all her cunning to that end. On the most obvious level, she steals her food. Otherwise, she repeatedly taunts her with sly observations about her daughters, sowing increasing doubts in Bernarda's mind. It is not without significance, therefore, that it should be Poncia who, towards the end of Act Two, informs Bernarda that Pepe el Romano has been seen at one of the windows at 'half-past four in the morning'. This is Poncia's moment of quiet triumph, due compensation for the way in which Bernarda has taunted her about her mother's dubious reputation. This said, Poncia shares many of Bernarda's attitudes, particularly in relation to traditional values. Her words to Adela in Act Two reveal a concern with good name and reputation which in many ways echoes that of her mistress: 'I want to live in a respectable house. I don't want to be disgraced in my old age!' In the end, however, we feel that Poncia has more genuine integrity than Bernarda.

The Servant

Lower than Poncia in the domestic hierarchy, the Servant has been and continues to be exploited by her masters, for if Bernarda's second husband has used her sexually in the past, she is abused in other ways by Bernarda in the present. But the harshness displayed towards her by Bernarda – 'Get out! This isn't your place' – is in turn directed by the Servant towards another less fortunate than herself: the Beggar Woman who in Act One comes looking for scraps. The Servant illustrates the point that in this household repression breeds repression, cruelty cruelty in an ever-widening circle. Less powerful and less cunning than Poncia, she is nevertheless influenced by her, and, like the older servant, is willing to strike back at Bernarda by stealing her food.

Prudencia

A neighbour of Bernarda and ten years younger, Prudencia is her complete opposite, for while the former rules with a rod of iron, Prudencia is caught in the midst of family problems, unable to control things: 'I let the water flow'. Her husband's quarrel with his brothers over an inheritance, as well as his anger with his daughter, have left her dispirited. In addition, she is depressed by increasing blindness, which will soon prevent her from going to church, her one remaining consolation. Like many Lorca characters, she appears only briefly, but is a figure of true pathos.

The play as tragedy

It has been suggested that, because *The House of Bernarda Alba* has a much greater social emphasis than *Blood Wedding*, it is also a different kind of tragedy. Herbert Ramsden, for example, has put forward the argument that in *Blood Wedding* fate dominates the lives of the characters, in particular the Bride and Leonardo, working upon their attraction to each other to bring about their misfortune, and he concludes therefore that passion is an internal pressure (*La casa de Bernarda Alba*, ed. H. Ramsden, pp. xxi–xxiii). In *The House of Bernarda Alba*, on the other hand, he argues that the pressures on Adela are not internal but external – a repression exerted by those traditional values and attitudes embodied in Bernarda and in the villagers, in short by the society in which she lives. My own belief is that, as far as the tragic process is concerned, there is not a fundamental difference between the two plays, for both conform to a pattern of tragedy characteristic of Lorca's work as a whole. Lorca's concept of tragedy has at its core the notion of aspiration, whatever form that takes, and that aspiration is characterised by its intensity and single-mindedness. Because different characters have different aspirations, it follows that desires and passions are frequently incompatible with and intolerant of the wishes of others, mutually exclusive, and that, because these passions are also deep-rooted and ineradicable, the characters themselves are inevitably set on a collision course whose outcome will be catastrophic. As far as the emotions of the audience are concerned, the spectacle is one which elicits both sympathy and, ultimately, pity. At the end of Lorca's tragedies, moreover, the spectator is left, not with a feeling of hope for the future, as is frequently the case in Shakespearean tragedy, but with a sense of hopelessness and no escape, obliged to face the awful truth of the way things are.

   The House of Bernarda Alba conforms to this pattern in every respect. The element of aspiration is embodied in Adela's longing for Pepe el Romano, which is as strong as the Bride's passion for Leonardo in *Blood Wedding*, but it is equally evident in Bernarda's resolve to maintain her family's good name. Both individuals pursue their objectives with utter single-mindedness, and these are, for that reason, mutually exclusive, for Adela's determination to enjoy Pepe el Romano involves precisely that rejection of the moral and social restraints which, in order to protect her reputation, Bernarda is resolved to uphold. In addition, Adela's passion for Pepe is as immovable as her mother's embracing of traditional values. In Adela's case, the passage of time and the new circumstances of Angustias's imminent marriage to Pepe have done nothing to diminish her long-standing sexual attraction to him: 'Looking into his eyes is just like slowly drinking his blood!' As for Bernarda, her concern with traditional values, including good name and reputation, is deeply ingrained in her, in part inherited from previous generations, in part a response to neighbours ever eager to malign both her and her children. From the outset, then, Adela and Bernarda, their respective paths mapped out, are bound for disaster. And even if the role of fate is less obvious and less theatrical here than in *Blood Wedding*, there is still throughout the play a strong sense of inevitability. In Act One Martirio observes of a friend: 'I can see that everything's a terrible repetition. Her fate is the same as her mother's and her grandmother's.' And when in Act Two she longs for the rain and the coolness of autumn, Amelia comments on the fact that summer will return: 'When it's gone it will soon come round again!'

   In terms of the tragic emotions, Adela has many qualities which invite sympathy and admiration. She is young and attractive and possesses a resolve which in her sisters has become despair and resignation. Bernarda does not, of course, invite the same kind of sympathy, but she too is determined, and, to the extent that she remains true to her beliefs, worthy of a certain admiration. As for pity, it is Adela who inspires this as we witness her growing inability to help herself in a situation which, step by step, leads to her destruction.

The ending of the play, like that of *Blood Wedding*, is characterised by a sense of hopelessness. Far from suggesting an end to a terrible situation and thus promise for the future, Adela's death signifies for her sisters a further period of mourning, a longer confinement in the house, another step in their journey to despair and even madness. It is the blackest of endings. If Adela's death leaves us with a sense of pity, the fate reserved for her sisters in the years ahead transforms that pity into terror.

Staging of Lorca's plays in his lifetime

The production of Lorca's first play, *The Butterfly's Evil Spell*, which opened at the Teatro Eslava in Madrid on 22 March 1920, was an unmitigated disaster. The original intention of the theatre impresario, Gregorio Martínez Sierra, was that the play should be performed by puppets, which might well have been more effective, but in the end it was presented by actors, the role of the Butterfly performed by the leading ballet dancer, Encarnación López Júlvez, 'La Argentina'. The set and costumes were extremely colourful and the music used at particular points in the play was by Grieg. From the outset a section of the audience, clearly hostile to any kind of experimentation in the theatre, seemed determined to ruin the evening, and the reviews which appeared in the following morning's newspapers were not much more encouraging.

Although Lorca worked on a number of puppet plays and farces between 1922 and 1927, his second production was *Mariana Pineda*, which he had completed in 1924, and which was premiered at the Teatro Goya in Barcelona on 24 June 1927, the eponymous heroine played by the famous actress Margarita Xirgu, who would become increasingly involved in Lorca's work, and the sets designed by Salvador Dalí. The play was performed only six times in Barcelona, for Margarita Xirgu's company ended their season there on 28 June, but it was warmly received by the critics, as was the case when the production opened in the following autumn at the Teatro Fontalba in Madrid. Contemporary reviews of the Madrid production emphasise both the highly poetic nature of Lorca's treatment of the historical subject, so familiar to Spaniards, and the stylisation of the production in which sets and costumes played such an important part. M. Fernández-Almagro, the theatre critic of the newspaper, *La Voz*, spoke of the exquisite simplicity of Dalí's designs, a view echoed by E. Díez-Canedo in *El Sol*. In short, despite the fact that *Mariana Pineda* was a historical play and therefore open to a Naturalistic treatment, Lorca's poetic approach to it, underlined by the production itself, points to the general thrust of his theatre as a whole.

It was again Margarita Xirgu who played the lead part in the premiere of *The Shoemaker's Wonderful Wife* at the Teatro Español in Madrid on 24 December 1930. Particularly interesting about this production was the fact that Lorca himself, dressed in a star-spangled cloak, read the prologue in which the Author appears on stage and informs the audience of the need for poetry and magic on the contemporary stage. In terms of its staging, the play evidently put into practice Lorca's intentions, for the sets and costumes, based on drawings by the dramatist himself, and influenced by Picasso's designs for Manuel de Falla's *The Three-Cornered Hat*, matched the character of the play in their bold, vibrant colours and combined perfectly with vigorous movement and language in order to recreate on the modern stage all the vitality of a long puppet-play tradition. Lorca's piece ran for some thirty performances and greatly strengthened his working relationship with Margarita Xirgu.

The spring of 1933 saw two triumphant premieres which increased Lorca's fame as a playwright: *Blood Wedding* at the Teatro Beatriz in Madrid on 8 March, and *The Love of Don Perlimplín for Belisa in his Garden* on 5 April at the Teatro Español, both directed by Lorca himself. Lorca's work was now being influenced greatly by his own experience as a director with the touring company, 'La Barraca', which provided him with an ever deepening knowledge of the practicalities of performance. The reviews of *The Love of Don Perlimplín* point to the colourful stylisation of the production, enhanced by the music of Scarlatti.

At the end of May 1933 the Madrid production of *Blood Wedding* opened in Barcelona, and in July another production of the play was a great success in Buenos Aires before going on tour and returning to the city in October. It ran for several months, made Lorca a good deal of money and established his reputation in Argentina. In December, moreover, the same company opened with *The Shoemaker's Wonderful Wife*, which proved to be equally successful.

Lola Membrives, whose company produced both plays in Buenos Aires, was anxious to stage another play of Lorca's in early 1934, and, in the absence of a new work, decided to present *Mariana Pineda*, which opened on 12 January. In spite of the fact that the famous actress took the part of Mariana, this early play of Lorca's was compared unfavourably with *Blood Wedding* and the production was not a great success. In contrast, *Yerma*, the second play in his rural trilogy, was a complete triumph when it opened on 29 December at the Teatro Español in Madrid, with Margarita Xirgu in the title role. Initially, right-wing extremists, enraged by Lorca's homosexuality and left-wing sympathies, as well as by Margarita Xirgu's support for Manuel Azaña, a leading left-wing politician who had recently been imprisoned, attempted to disrupt the performance, but were then thrown out of the theatre. When the curtain fell, the reaction of the audience was rapturous, and Lorca himself was obliged to make numerous appearances on stage. Writing in *El Sol* the following day, M. Fernández-Almagro spoke of the dramatist's stark, classical treatment of his subject matter, of Margarita Xirgu's instinctive feeling for every nuance of emotion and gesture on the part of the protagonist, and of the way in which the stage-design by Manuel Fontanals enhanced and harmonised with the action throughout. With regard to the latter, Enrique Díez-Canedo, writing in *La Voz*, referred to Fontanal's broad effects, lacking in fussy realistic details, which formed the background to the action. And, as for the play itself, he drew attention to the important point that no one should fall into the trap of regarding Lorca's writing as Naturalistic. It is, above all, poetic, but its poetry is strong and vibrant, without sentimentality.

1935 saw a number of important productions of Lorca's plays in Spain. While *Yerma* continued at the Teatro Español, the company of Lola Membrives had returned from Buenos Aires and on 28 February opened at the Madrid Coliseum with her production of

Blood Wedding. Less than a month later the company, giving two performances each evening as was the Spanish practice, gave *Blood Wedding* at the first performance and *The Shoemaker's Wonderful Wife* at the second. In the first quarter of 1935 Lorca therefore had three plays running in Madrid, an unheard-of event in the theatre of that time. By the middle of the year he had also finished writing *Doña Rosita the Spinster*, which Margarita Xirgu proposed to include in her forthcoming season in Barcelona. The season of one month at the Teatro Barcelona opened on 10 September with a production of Lorca's adaptation of Lope de Vega's *The Foolish Lady*, followed a week later by *Yerma*, the success of which was as great as it had been in Madrid. On 5 November the company performed *Yerma* at the Teatro Principal in Valencia, the second production in a short season there, and then returned to Barcelona where Margarita Xirgu would present both *Blood Wedding* and *Doña Rosita the Spinster* at the Principal Palace Theatre. The former opened on 22 November to great acclaim, the sets designed by José Caballero and the music directed by Lorca who also accompanied on the piano the lullaby in the second scene of Act One. If anything, the premiere of *Doña Rosita the Spinster* on 12 December was an even greater success. In this play, set in Granada, and in which, over a period of twenty-five years, Rosita waits in vain for her fiancé to return while hope gradually gives way to a realisation of the hopelessness of her situation, Lorca had evoked both his own experience of love and the beautiful, magical, sad and introverted city in which he had spent so much of his life. Essentially different from *Blood Wedding* and *Yerma* in its subject matter, *Doña Rosita the Spinster* has something of the bitter-sweetness of Chekhov, a point not lost on the critics who praised it the following day. Writing in *La Vanguardia*, María Luz Rosales commented in particular on the way in which the play induced laughter and tears at the same time, and on how, through both prose and poetry, the mood of Granada through a quarter of a century is so delicately and evocatively created by the writer. In Barcelona Lorca's play was performed to packed houses, regular articles about him appeared in the newspapers, a special performance of the play was put on for the flower-sellers of the Ramblas, and at the end of the year there was a magnificent banquet at the Majestic Inglaterra Hotel, attended by Catalonia's artists and intellectuals. Lorca was indeed at the height of his fame.

In January 1936 Margarita Xirgu left Spain for Cuba, where on 16 February she presented *Yerma* in Havana to enthusiastic audiences. On 18 April she opened her season in Mexico with the same play and subsequently presented *Doña Rosita the Spinster*, *The Shoemaker's Wonderful Wife* and *Blood Wedding*. In Spain itself there were to be no further productions of Lorca's plays during that year, although he was at work, as always, on a variety of projects. What is surprising is not simply the extent to which he was always eager to experiment but the fact that such an innovative dramatist should also have triumphed in the commercial theatre of his day.

Production history of *The House of Bernarda Alba*

The premiere

Given the circumstances of Lorca's death and the terrible nature of the Spanish Civil War and its aftermath, *The House of Bernarda Alba* did not receive its first performance until 1945, nine years after its completion. Although there seems to have been a production in Spain by a company called 'La Carátula' in March 1945, the official premiere took place in Buenos Aires where it opened on 8 March, with Margarita Xirgu playing the role of Bernarda Alba. She chose the fifteen other actresses with great care, for in her own words she wished to establish clearly 'the psychology of each character, giving it its true humanity'. The sets were designed by Santiago Ontañón, a close friend of Lorca who had been his set-designer for the premiere of *Blood Wedding* in 1933, as well as for other projects.

The production proved to be a great success. As the curtain fell, the applause was instantaneous and Margarita Xirgu came on stage to address the audience: 'He [Lorca] wanted this play to be premiered here, and so it has been, but he wanted to be present and destiny has prevented it. Destiny, which brings such sorrow to the lives of so many. A curse on war!' Immediately, the stage was covered with flowers, the homage, as the newspapers described it, of the Buenos Aires public to a great writer and a great actress. Writing in *La Nación* the following morning, the theatre critic of the Buenos Aires daily observed that Margarita Xirgu had brought to the part of Bernarda all the authority of her voice and bearing;

that María Gámez had revealed great psychological insight in the
part of Poncia; and that Isabel Pradas showed increasing
confidence as Adela. Adding that the success of the production as
a whole lay in its ensemble acting, effectively directed by
Margarita Xirgu herself, this critic's one reservation was that the
whiteness of the sets clashed, he felt, with the gloomy nature of
the house and its inhabitants. However, the stage directions
suggest that Lorca intended this effect in order to produce a
greater contrast.

Spanish productions

The first major production of the play in Spain took place in 1964
in Madrid, where it opened at the Teatro Goya on 10 January,
directed by Juan Antonio Bardem and designed by Antonio Saura,
brother of Carlos Saura, the now famous film-director. In his
notes for the production, Bardem makes some very interesting
observations on various aspects of the play: in particular, that
there should be great emphasis on the extent to which the rooms
in the house are isolated from the world outside it. In addition,
the three different locations for each act should suggest a
movement further and deeper into the house, reinforcing the
isolation of the women, and the walls in each case should be very
high, creating the effect of a well in which the characters are
imprisoned. As for the lighting, Bardem suggests that it should be
constant within each act and should change only when light
comes in from outside, as in the case of an outside door being
opened, suggesting thereby the existence of the world from which
the women are cut off.

  As far as the characters are concerned, Bardem notes that
Bernarda should be the very personification of authority, using her
stick and her cold smile to assert it. At the same time, she should
raise her voice only at particular moments when her authority is
threatened. Even when she sees Adela's body, the cry she utters
should be brief, for it is important that she recover and assert her
authority quickly. As for Poncia, Bardem suggests that she serves
Bernarda without being at all servile. Although she is typical of
her class, she should never be presented as a stereotype, and she
should not be over-demonstrative, for women from the Spanish
countryside rarely display their emotions through excessive gesture

or movement. The daughters, Bardem believes, should be individualised as much as possible, but he disagrees with Lorca in relation to the way in which they should be dressed, arguing that in Act Three Martirio should appear in black, Amelia, Angustias and Magdalena in a mixture of black and white, and Adela entirely in white. Bernarda should be dressed in black throughout the play.

Reviewing the production in *ABC* the morning after the opening, Enrique Llovet considered Lorca's play to be a powerful modern tragedy which, at the same time, echoed the great Spanish playwrights of the seventeenth century, in particular Lope de Vega and Calderón. A year later the same production opened at the Teatro Principal in Zaragoza. Writing in the *Heraldo de Aragón*, Pablo Cistue de Castro drew attention to the effectiveness of the contrast between the whiteness of the walls and the black costumes worn by the women, and to the economy of gesture and the vocal control employed by Candida Losada in the part of Bernarda. Above all, he praised the 'stylised realism' which Bardem, the director, brought to the production.

Twenty years later, in the autumn of 1984, *The House of Bernarda Alba* was directed at the Teatro Español in Madrid – the theatre in which several of Lorca's plays had been presented in his lifetime – by José Carlos Plaza, who nine years earlier had worked on a much more experimental approach to the play. As in the case of the 1964 production, the director's notes again throw valuable light on the interpretation of the play. The sets, by Andrea D'Odorico, were intended to suggest a labyrinth, a succession of rooms and corridors in which one individual could easily spy on another, while the walls should be high and cold; glass in the doors should draw attention both to the private world of the daughters' bedrooms and to the outside world where Pepe el Romano and the reapers rule. In general the house should be presented very realistically in a way which emphasises Bernarda's wealth, but with peeling walls which also point to age and decay. The contrast between black and white, which is often exaggerated in productions of the play, should be avoided. In this context, the lighting of the stage plays a crucial part. The light should come from outside and in Act One should come from the courtyard or

patio, filtering through the corridors of the house into the room
where the women are gathered. Act Two should be set in the
same room, at three o'clock in the afternoon when the heat is
suffocating, and the lighting should suggest that, as well as
sensuality, violence and intimacy. Act Three, set in the courtyard
at night, is, however, entirely different, and when the oil-lamp on
the table is extinguished, the lighting has to be that of a summer's
night.

As for the characters, Carlos Plaza saw Bernarda as a woman
whose first marriage had been arranged and who, the second time
round, had married for love a man somewhat below her in social
class. His subsequent adventures with other women of his own
kind have left her embittered towards them and over-protective of
her daughters, even though they represent her failure to give
birth to a son, a further source of disappointment. Angustias, the
child of the first marriage, is unloved by Bernarda because of it
and has been increasingly distanced from her mother with the
passage of time. Martirio is marginalised by her physical defects,
which in turn lie at the root of her envy of Adela. Although she is
younger than Amelia, Martirio has succeeded in enlisting her
support. Eventually she will be a greater monster than Bernarda
herself. Amelia, in contrast, is passive, rarely in the foreground,
and seeks to avoid any problems. Magdalena is the daughter who
most feels her father's death. She also has a sense of irony, which
explains her pessimism about her future. Adela, in contrast, is the
most positive, determined to have her own way, but she does not
think of the possible consequences.

Carlos Plaza's production was generally considered by the critics
to be less stylised than Bardem's. Writing in *Cultura*, José Monleón
drew attention to its 'realism' and to the minute detail with which
each scene and each character was presented. Similarly, E. Haro
Teglen, in *El País*, spoke of the 'masterly realism' of the stage-
design and of the way in which the cast – the role of Bernarda
was played by Berta Riaza – successfully worked within this
'theatrical naturalism'. Both these productions are interesting
because of their directors' views on the 'realism' of the staging and
the psychology of the characters. They clearly suggest the different
possibilities open to other directors.

American and British productions
One of the earliest American productions of the play took place in
January 1951 at the ANTA Theater (American National Theater
and Academy) where it ran for seventeen performances, and in
which the role of Bernarda was played by Katrina Paxinou. In
1960 it received a television production in which Anne Revere
played Bernarda, Eileen Heckart Poncia and Suzanne Pleshette
Adela. Three years later, in the autumn of 1963, a highly
successful production was presented at the Encore Theater in San
Francisco by the Actors' Workshop, directed by Lee Brewster.
Reviewing the production in the *San Francisco Examiner* on 17
September, Stanley Eichelbaum drew attention both to the visual
impact of the production and the outstanding quality of the
language. Much less 'poetic' in this respect than *Blood Wedding*, it
had a more immediate appeal for American audiences who, when
the latter received its American premiere in 1935, were reduced to
laughter by some of Lorca's imagery.

During the 1970s three productions in Spanish were staged in
New York. The first of these took place at the ADAL Theater in
February 1972 and was enthusiastically received. Two years later
the production at Nuestro Teatro was acclaimed by a reviewer
writing in *Show Business* for the universality of Lorca's vision as a
dramatist. And when the play was staged by the Repertorio
Español in 1979, Richard Shepard, in the *New York Times*, was
impressed by the strength of the production. Ten years later, in
the spring/summer of 1989, the same company staged the play
again in New York, leading one of the theatre reviewers of the
New York Times to observe that with the passage of time *The House
of Bernarda Alba* had lost none of its relevance.

As far as Britain is concerned, major productions of the play
did not take place until the 1970s, the explanation for this
probably being the absence of suitable English translations. On 21
March 1973, a version of the play by Tom Stoppard, directed by
Robin Phillips, opened at the Greenwich Theatre in London.
Bernarda was played by June Jago, Poncia by Patience Collier,
and Adela by Mia Farrow. Writing in the summer edition of
Drama, J. W. Lambert noted that in general the production
succeeded in projecting the play as 'a metaphor of the human
spirit shackled by an outworn creed', but he also had particular
reservations about the set, the accents and the version. The design

by Daphne Dare employed the black walls of the theatre as a contrast to one white wall and floor, and contained too a heavy door and an iron grille. The lighting consisted of 'individual spots giving pools of brilliance and shadowed corners'. This attempt at stylisation was, in Lambert's opinion, offset by the fact that 'the use of white plastic . . . imparted a faintly science-fiction air'. The accents too posed a problem in the sense that, as far as Bernarda and the daughters were concerned, they were too well-groomed and required 'some roughening of a regional kind', though the peformances were good, for June Jago 'gave Bernarda all the necessary strength', Mia Farrow 'made us feel Adela's anguish burning in her flesh', and Patience Collier created a 'splendidly creased old Poncia'. As for Tom Stoppard's version, Lambert describes it as 'too often free and easy . . . e.g. Bernarda's first tyrannical word to her seething daughters is "Silence!", and could not possibly be "Shut up!"'

By far the most celebrated British production of the play to date is that which opened at the Lyric Theatre, Hammersmith, London, on 8 September 1986, and then transferred to the West End, where it opened at the Globe Theatre on 16 January 1987. The production was directed by the Spanish actress and director, Nuria Espert, and had Glenda Jackson in the role of Bernarda and Joan Plowright as Poncia. Michael Billington's review of the Lyric production in the *Guardian* on 10 September 1986 was highly approving in almost every respect. The single set, by Ezio Frigerio, which consisted of 'towering, white, age-pocked Granada walls inset with tiny, barred windows and culminating in a grating, flagstone floor', conveyed simultaneously 'a prison courtyard, a nunnery and an asylum', and 'the claustrophobia is heightened by the lowering space and by Franca Squarciatino's black costumes giving the women the look of bottled insects'. As for the performances, Billington singled out Glenda Jackson's 'tyrannical matriarch who rules over her brood like a female leopard (she even brandishes a claw at a recalcitrant daughter) and who howls with sadistic relish as an errant village woman is dragged through the streets'. Joan Plowright gave 'a marvellous performance . . . : she is earthy, robust, sensual, but the way she smooths the nap of the folded linen evokes a lifetime of drudgery'. As for Patricia Hayes, 'stark naked in a white shift', she 'gives a highly courageous performance as the mad, locked-in grandmother'. Of the transfer to the West End, Billington noted in the *Guardian* on 14 January 1987 that 'what this magnificent play shows is how realism can be elevated to the poetic level'.

This view was shared by many other critics, but there were, too, dissenting voices. Of the production as a whole, Christopher Edwards observed in the *Spectator* that it had 'a cold, scrupulous, Nordic feel to it as if the cast (in particular Glenda Jackson as the repressive Spanish matriarch) have understood from an *intellectual* point of view what Lorca is saying but lack the resources to embody the passions that are there in the play', a view shared by Andrew Rissik in the *Independent*. And while Eric Shorter, writing in the *Daily Telegraph*, admired much, he also noted that 'the voices remain those of an English theatrical drawing-room – well bred, beautifully enunciated, highly intelligent but stuck, so to say, in Professor Higgins' territory rather than Lorca's'. Of the central role, Martin Hoyle in the *Financial Times* felt that 'Glenda Jackson is too young. Ramrod-rigid, her voice harsh, the most passionately committed of our actresses tries to compensate with sheer intensity', while Jim Hiley in the *Listener* noted that 'Glenda Jackson's ramrod-backed, singsong matriarch remains, until her peculiarly unmoving final agonies'.

The differing critical reactions to this production allow certain important conclusions to be drawn. Firstly, it did not take into account the implication of Lorca's stage-directions that each act of the play moves its action deeper into the house, progressively isolating the women from the outside world. Secondly, there are clear pointers to over-acting in the central role of Bernarda – 'she even brandishes a claw ... howls with sadistic relish', 'peculiarly unmoving final agonies' – which contradict the view of the Spanish director, Juan Antonio Bardem, that she should rarely raise her voice and that, even when she sees Adela's body, her cry should be brief. In this respect the performance of Bernarda by Irene Gutiérrez Caba in the 1987 film version of the play, directed by Mario Camus, is exemplary and should be observed by any actress who aspires to play the part. Finally, the comment that in the Lyric/Globe staging 'the voices remain those of an English theatrical drawing-room' underlines a common fault in English productions of the play.

Though much less widely reviewed, the production which opened at the Nottingham Playhouse on 28 February 1991,

directed by Pip Broughton, may have been more successful in
certain respects. Michael Schmidt noted in the *Daily Telegraph* on 3
March that 'Simon Vincenzi's sets – all white walls and angles –
are drenched with a merciless sunlight'. The reference to 'sets'
suggests, at least, more than one location, 'angles' the labyrinthine
nature of the house, though there also seems to be excessive
sunlight within. In the *Independent* on 14 March, Jeffrey Wainwright
drew attention to Bernarda's daughters 'struck in black against the
pitiless white walls', which suggests that in this production Lorca's
black and white contrast was preserved. Of the performances
Schmidt felt that Rosalind Knight in the role of Bernarda 'moves
about warily, like a scorpion, ready to use her walking-stick on
daughters and servants. But her cold, appraising gaze and her
heartlessly perfect diction are more to be feared than her physical
wrath'. Wainwright, in contrast, believed that the performance did
not capture sufficiently 'the more awful dimension of her
psychological power'. But both critics agreed that the roles of the
daughters were well played – Helena Bonham-Carter played
Adela – and that the production as a whole was powerful.

   The smallest British theatre to have staged *The House of Bernarda
Alba* is the Gate Theatre, London, where it opened on 9 October
1992, directed by Katie Mitchell. Andrew St George, reviewing the
production in the *Financial Times*, noted that the 'small theatre
refashions the claustrophobia of Lorca's *mise-en-scène*: a *hacienda*,
walls dark in the midday heat, shafts of light striking into the
gloom'. As far as the interpretation of Lorca's text is concerned,
Mitchell introduced a number of touches of her own: a suggestion
of incest between Amelia and Martirio; a linking of the events of
the play to the Fascism of the 1930s; and an attempt to relate
Adela to the crucified Christ by means of a tableau evoking
Leonardo da Vinci's *The Last Supper*. Claire Armistead observed in
the *Guardian* that there were times 'when the symbolism seems to
outweigh textually rooted characterisation', but in general there
was considerable praise both for individual performances and for
the production as a whole. For Rick Jones in *Time Out*, Dinah
Stabb's Bernarda was 'a powerful performance – brutal, hard,
rigid', though for Claire Armistead she was not extreme enough.
Graham Hassell in *What's On* observed that the daughters 'are
sharply drawn by a mesmeric cast'. Of the production as a whole,
Michael Coveney concluded in the *Observer*: 'For all the stately

grandeur of the Glenda Jackson/Joan Plowright revival some years ago, this version throbs more vibrantly with the tragic waste of unfulfilled sexuality as the household buckles down for another extended period of fruitless mourning.'

The translation

There are various problems associated with translating Lorca's plays into English but the translator should seek above all to recreate the 'world' of a Lorca play. This demands familiarity with that world, with its customs as well as its language, and necessitates that he/she should keep the translation as close to the original Spanish as possible. *The House of Bernarda Alba* is full of allusions to the customs and the culture of southern Spain, all of which combine to create the particular world which the characters inhabit. As for Lorca's language, this play does not contain the highly poetic passages which distinguish, for instance, *Blood Wedding*, but its prose dialogue is equally spare and concise – something the translation should strive to preserve.

The first translation of *The House of Bernarda Alba*, by James Graham-Luján and Richard L. O'Connell, was published by New Directions in 1945 in New York and issued in the United Kingdom by Penguin Books in *Three Tragedies*. In 1987 this translation was replaced by that of Michael Dewell and Carmen Zapata, which was published in the United States in *The Rural Trilogy*, and subsequently issued in the United Kingdom by Penguin in *Three Plays*. Both translations have, of course, a marked American tone and both translate the original Spanish fairly literally.

Among other translations, some have been commissioned by theatres from writers or translators who may have little or no knowledge of Spanish and who often base them on literal translations prepared by others or on existing published versions. In such circumstances it is not surprising that such 'translations' should contain many errors or that there should be in the end, when these errors are frequent, a general 'watering down' of the Spanish original, a weakening of its true meaning and power. A number of examples clarify this point.

In Act One Bernarda claims that the poor soon forget their

troubles 'in front of a plateful of chickpeas'. In one of the
'translations' mentioned above, the phrase becomes 'over a plate
of beans', the characteristically Spanish dish replaced by something
much more general. Similarly, Poncia's description of Adela in Act
Two as someone who acts 'as if she had a lizard between her
breasts' – an extremely suggestive sexual allusion – becomes 'as if
she had a lizard down her dress', which merely suggests
squirming. And Bernarda's description in Act One of men
drooling over juicy gossip – 'they like to see it and talk about it
and suck their fingers when it happens' – becomes the much
weaker 'they like to watch and pass remarks and blow on their
fingers over it'. In short, there is in such a process both a
movement away from the specificity of the 'world' of the play and
a weakening of Lorca's powerful images. In addition, there are
many mistranslations: 'dirt floors' for 'huts of mud'; 'I didn't ask
you to repeat it' for 'I chose not to answer you'; 'in a really deep
voice' for 'he said very quietly'; 'Now run along with you' for
'Get out!'; and 'While I keep my eyes skinned' for 'my vigilance'.
It goes without saying that in such circumstances the art of
translation becomes a very approximate affair.

The translation presented here aims to be as faithful as possible
to the original Spanish and to provide a text which works on the
stage. Amongst Spanish dramatists of the twentieth century, Lorca
is the master of terse, concise dialogue, as though his characters
were often engaging in verbal table-tennis. This translation seeks,
therefore, to capture the essential confrontational quality of his
language. On the other hand, the syntax and rhythm of some of
Lorca's longer sentences, as well as particular Spanish phrases, do
not always transpose easily into English, and in these cases it is
necessary to make some adjustments. But in general the intention
is to provide a translation of the play which will be useful to
actors and to students of Lorca.

The Spanish text

The Spanish text used here is based on the manuscript version of
La casa de Bernarda Alba published in 1981 by Mario Hernández
(Alianza, Madrid). Before this, all editions were based on a text
first published in 1946 in Buenos Aires by the Editorial Losada,

which was subsequently found to contain many differences from
Lorca's own manuscript. Many of these differences are small but
some are quite significant. In the Losada text, for example, Poncia
observes of Magdalena after the first few lines of Act One: 'Era la
única que quería al padre' ('She was the only one who loved her
father'), while the Hernández text reads: 'Era a la única que
quería el padre' ('She was the only one her father loved'). The
difference of meaning is clearly important, since in the first case
Magdalena might love her father but remain unloved, while in the
second case she is clearly much loved: for the interpretation of her
role in the play, this relationship is crucial. The Hernández text,
therefore, is altogether superior to the earlier one – as the Notes
to this volume confirm – and the closest to Lorca's original
intentions.

Further reading

Plays by Lorca in English translation

Lorca Plays: One (*Blood Wedding* [*Bodas de sangre*] and *Doña Rosita the Spinster* [*Doña Rosita la soltera*], tr. Gwynne Edwards, and *Yerma*, tr. Peter Luke), London, Methuen, 1987

Lorca Plays: Two (*The Shoemaker's Wonderful Wife* [*La zapatera prodigiosa*], *The Love of Don Perlimplín* [*Amor de Don Perlimplín*], *The Puppet Show of Don Cristóbal* [*El retablillo de Don Cristóbal*], *The Butterfly's Evil Spell* [*El maleficio de la mariposa*], and *When Five Years Pass* [*Así que pasen cinco años*], tr. Gwynne Edwards), London, Methuen, 1990

Lorca Plays: Three (*Mariana Pineda* and *Play without a Title* [*Comedia sin título*], tr. Gwynne Edwards, and *The Public* [*El público*], tr. Henry Livings), London, Methuen, 1994

Full-length studies on Lorca

Adams, Mildred, *García Lorca: Playwright and Poet*, New York, George Braziller, 1977. An informal biography based on personal reminiscence.

Allen, Rupert C., *Psyche and Symbol in the Theatre of Federico García Lorca*, Austin and London, University of Texas Press, 1974. A dense analysis of Lorca's theatre in terms of its symbolism and psychological meaning.

Anderson, Reed, *Federico García Lorca*, London, Macmillan, 1984. A useful study of Lorca's theatre as a whole.

Binding, Paul, *Lorca: The Gay Imagination*, London, Gay Men's Press, 1985. An examination of Lorca's work from a gay perspective.

Busette, Cedric, *Obra dramática de García Lorca: Estudio de su configuración*, New York, Las Américas Publishing Co., 1971. Emphasises the role of fate in the tragedies.

Byrd, Suzanne, *'La Barraca' and the Spanish National Theatre*, New

York, Ediciones Abra, 1975. A useful examination of Lorca's
work as director with his travelling theatre company.

Correa, Gustavo, *La poesía mítica de Federico García Lorca*, Madrid,
Editorial Gredos, 1975, 2nd edn. A detailed study of the role of
myth and Nature in Lorca's work as a whole.

Durán, Manuel, ed., *Lorca: A Collection of Critical Essays*, New Jersey,
Prentice Hall, 1962. Contains twelve essays on Lorca's poetry
and theatre by academics and creative writers.

Edwards, Gwynne, *Lorca: The Theatre Beneath the Sand*, London,
Marion Boyars, 1980. A comprehensive study of Lorca's theatre
which includes sections on staging.

Edwards, Gwynne, *Dramatists in Perspective: Spanish Theatre in the
Twentieth Century*, Cardiff, University of Wales Press, 1985.
Chapter 3 examines Lorca in the context of European theatre.

Frazier, Brenda, *La mujer en el teatro de Federico García Lorca*, Madrid,
Editorial Plaza Mayor, 1973. A sensible analysis of the role of
women in Lorca's theatre.

García Lorca, Francisco, tr. Christopher Maurer, *In the Green Room:
Memories of Federico*, London, Peter Owen, 1989. Contains
reminiscences of theatre productions as well as analyses of plays.

Gibson, Ian, *Federico García Lorca: A Life*, London, Faber and Faber,
1989. An authoritative biography.

González del Valle, Luis, *La tragedia en el teatro de Unamuno, Valle-
Inclán y García Lorca*, New York, Torres, 1975. A general survey
of the tragic character of Lorca's major plays, with perceptive
observations.

Higginbotham, Virginia, *The Comic Spirit of Federico García Lorca*,
Austin, University of Texas Press, 1976. Concentrates on Lorca's
theatre within the context of puppet plays and farces.

Honig, Edwin, *García Lorca*, New York, New Directions, 1963. A
general introduction to Lorca's work.

Lima, Robert, *The Theater of García Lorca*, New York, Las Américas
Publishing Co., 1963. A detailed study with particular emphasis
on fate.

Martínez Nadal, Rafael, *Lorca's 'The Public': A Study of his Unfinished
Play (El Público) and of Love and Death in the Work of Federico García
Lorca*, London, Calder and Boyars, 1974. A wide-ranging and
dense study of Lorca's work as a whole, in particular his most
difficult play, *The Public*.

Morla Lynch, Carlos, *En España con Federico García Lorca: Páginas de*

un diario íntimo, 1928–36, Madrid, Editorial Aguilar, 1958.
Contains personal reminiscences and interesting background
material to Lorca's work.

Morris, C. Brian, *García Lorca, 'La casa de Bernarda Alba',* Critical
Guides to Spanish Texts, London, Grant and Cutler, 1990. A
detailed study of various aspects of the play.

Piasecki, Andy, *File on Lorca,* London, Methuen, 1991. One of the
Methuen Writer-Files series. Contains synopses of Lorca's plays,
as well as observations taken from various sources, including
reviews of productions.

Rodrigo, Antonina, *Margarita Xirgu y su teatro,* Barcelona, Editorial
Planeta, 1974. An informative study of the life and work of
Lorca's leading actress.

Sáenz de la Calzeda, Luis, *'La Barraca': Teatro Universitario,* Madrid,
Biblioteca de la Revista de Occidente, 1976. A detailed account
of Lorca's experiences with his travelling theatre company.

Smoot, Jean J., *A Comparison of Plays by John Millington Synge and
Federico García Lorca: The Poets and Time,* Madrid: Ediciones José
Porrúa Turanzas, 1978. Studies in particular the parallels
between Lorca's three rural tragedies and some of the plays of
Synge.

Short studies of *The House of Bernarda Alba*

Alvarez de Altman, Grace, 'Charactonyms in García Lorca's *House
of Bernarda Alba* (Sexual nihilism within the typology of literary
onomastics)', *Onomástica Canadiana,* 46 (1972), pp. 3–11

Anderson, A., 'The strategy of García Lorca's dramatic
composition 1930–1936', *Romance Quarterly,* 33 (1986), pp. 211–29

Anderson, Farris, *'La casa de Bernarda Alba*: Problems in Act One',
García Lorca Review, 5 (1977), pp. 66–80

Bardem, J. A., notes on the play in F. G. Lorca, *La casa de
Bernarda Alba,* Barcelona, Editorial Ayma, 1964

Belamich, A., *'El público* y *La casa de Bernarda Alba,* polos opuestos
en la dramaturgia de Lorca', in Ricardo Doménech (ed.), *'La
casa de Bernarda Alba' y el teatro de Lorca,* Madrid, Cátedra, 1985,
pp. 77–92

Bull, Judith M., ' "Santa Bárbara" and *La casa de Bernarda Alba',
Bulletin of Hispanic Studies,* 47 (1970), pp. 117–23

Burton, J., 'The greatest punishment: Female and male in Lorca's tragedies', in Beth Miller (ed.), *Women in Hispanic Literature: Icons and Fallen Idols*, Berkeley, University of California Press, 1983, pp. 259–79

Busette, C., 'Libido and repression in García Lorca's theatre', in James Redmond (ed.), *Drama, Sex and Politics*, Themes in Drama, 7, Cambridge University Press, 1985, pp. 173–82

Carlos Plaza, J., notes on the play in F. G. Lorca, *La casa de Bernarda Alba*, Madrid, Los Libros del Teatro Español, 1984

Crispin, J., '*La casa de Bernarda Alba* dentro de la visión mítica lorquiana', in Ricardo Doménech (ed.), '*La casa de Bernarda Alba* . . .', *op. cit.*, pp. 171–85

Doménech, R., 'Símbolo, mito y rito en *La casa de Bernarda Alba*', in Ricardo Doménech (ed.), '*La casa de Bernarda Alba* . . .', *op. cit.*, pp. 187–209

Edwards, G., 'The way things are: Towards a definition of Lorcan tragedy', *Anales de la literatura española contemporánea*, 21 (1996), pp. 271–90

Fiddian, R., 'Adelaida's story and the cyclical design of *La casa de Bernarda Alba*', *Romance Notes*, 21 (1980–1), pp. 150–4

Fraile, M., 'An introduction to *La casa de Bernarda Alba*', *Vida Hispánica*, 22, 1 (Winter 1974), pp. 5–15

Galerstein, Carolyn, 'The political power of Bernarda Alba', in James Redmond (ed.), *Drama, Sex and Politics*, *op. cit.*, pp. 183–90

García-Posada, M., 'Realidad y transfiguración artística en *La casa de Bernarda Alba*', in Ricardo Doménech (ed.), '*La casa de Bernarda Alba* . . .', *op. cit.*, pp. 149–70

Greenfield, S., 'Poetry and stagecraft in *La casa de Bernarda Alba*', *Hispania* (USA), 38 (1955), pp. 456–61

Havard, R. G., 'The hidden parts of Bernarda Alba', *Romance Notes*, 26 (1985), pp. 102–8

Hernández, M., introduction to his edition of *La casa de Bernarda Alba*, Madrid, Alianza, 1981

Hickey, L., 'Culturology and cumulativeness in *La casa de Bernarda Alba*', *Quinquereme*, 5 (1982), pp. 186–95

Josephs, A., and Caballero, C., introduction to their edition of *La casa de Bernarda Alba*, Madrid, Cátedra, 1978

Morris, C. B., *García Lorca, 'La casa de Bernarda Alba'*, Critical Guides to Spanish Texts, London, Grant and Cutler, 1970

Newberry, Wilma, 'Patterns of negation in *La casa de Bernarda*

Alba', *Hispania* (USA), 59 (1976), pp. 802–9

Ramsden, H., introduction to his edition of *La casa de Bernarda Alba*, Manchester University Press, 1983

Rubia Barcia, J., 'El realismo "mágico" de *La casa de Bernarda Alba*', *Revista Hispánica Moderna*, 31 (1965), pp. 385–98

Sánchez, R. G., 'La última manera dramática de García Lorca (hacia una clarificación de lo "social" en su teatro)', *Papeles de Son Armadans*, 178 (1971), pp. 83–102

Seybolt, R. A., 'Characterization in *La casa de Bernarda Alba*: The case of Martirio', *García Lorca Review*, 8 (1980), pp. 82–90

Wells, C. M., 'The natural norm in the plays of F. García Lorca', *Hispanic Review*, 38 (1970), pp. 299–313

Yndurán, F., '*La casa de Bernarda Alba*, ensayo de interpretación', in Ricardo Doménech (ed.), '*La casa de Bernarda Alba . . .*', *op. cit.*, pp. 123–47

Young, R. A., 'García Lorca's *La casa de Bernarda Alba*: A microcosm of Spanish culture', *Modern Languages*, 50 (1969), pp. 66–72

Ziomek, H., 'El simbolismo del blanco en *La casa de Bernarda Alba* y en *La Dama del Alba*', *Symposium*, XXIV (1970), pp. 81–5

The House of Bernarda Alba
A Drama of Women in the Villages of Spain

La casa de Bernarda Alba
Drama de mujeres en los pueblos de España

Translated by Gwynne Edwards

BERNARDA, *60 años*
MARÍA JOSEFA, *madre de Bernarda, 80 años*
ANGUSTIAS, *hija de Bernarda, 39 años*
MAGDALENA, *hija de Bernarda, 30 años*
AMELIA, *hija de Bernarda, 27 años*
MARTIRIO, *hija de Bernarda, 24 años*
ADELA, *hija de Bernarda, 20 años*
CRIADA, *50 años*
LA PONCIA, *criada, 60 años*
PRUDENCIA, *50 años*
MENDIGA *con* NIÑA
MUJERES DE LUTO
MUJER 1
MUJER 2
MUJER 3
MUJER 4
MUCHACHA

El poeta advierte que estos tres actos tienen la intención de un documental fotográfico.

CHARACTERS

BERNARDA, *aged 60*
MARÍA JOSEFA, *Bernarda's mother, aged 80*
ANGUSTIAS, *Bernarda's daughter, aged 39*
MAGDALENA, *Bernarda's daughter, aged 30*
AMELIA, *Bernarda's daughter, aged 27*
MARTIRIO, *Bernarda's daughter, aged 24*
ADELA, *Bernarda's daughter, aged 20*
SERVANT, *aged 50*
PONCIA, *servant, aged 60*
PRUDENCIA, *aged 50*
BEGGAR WOMAN *and her* LITTLE GIRL
WOMEN MOURNERS
FIRST WOMAN
SECOND WOMAN
THIRD WOMAN
FOURTH WOMAN
GIRL

The poet points out that these three acts are intended to be a photographic documentary.

Acto Primero

Habitación blanquísima del interior de la casa de BER-NARDA. *Muros gruesos. Puertas en arco con cortinas de yute rematadas con madroños y volantes. Sillas de anea. Cuadros con paisajes inverosímiles de ninfas o reyes de leyenda. Es verano. Un gran silencio umbroso se extiende por la escena. Al levantarse el telón está la escena sola. Se oyen doblar las campanas.*

Sale la CRIADA.

CRIADA. Ya tengo el doble de esas campanas metido entre las sienes.

PONCIA (*sale comiendo chorizo y pan*). Llevan ya más de dos horas de gori-gori. Han venido curas de todos los pueblos. La iglesia está hermosa. En el primer responso se desmayó la Magdalena.

CRIADA. Esa es la que se queda más sola.

PONCIA. Era a la única que quería el padre. ¡Ay! ¡Gracias a Dios que estamos solas un poquito! Yo he venido a comer.

CRIADA. ¡Si te viera Bernarda!

PONCIA. ¡Quisiera que ahora, como no come ella, que todas nos muriéramos de hambre! ¡Mandona! ¡Domi-nanta! ¡Pero se fastidia! Le he abierto la orza de chorizos.

CRIADA (*con tristeza ansiosa*). ¿Por qué no me das para mi niña, Poncia?

PONCIA. Entra y llévate también un puñado de garbanzos. ¡Hoy no se dará cuenta!

VOZ (*dentro*). ¡Bernarda!

PONCIA. La vieja. ¿Está bien encerrada?

Act One

A very white inner room in BERNARDA's *house. Thick walls. Arched doorways with jute curtains edged with tassels and flounces. Rush-bottomed chairs. Paintings of unrealistic landscapes with nymphs or legendary kings. It is summer. A great brooding silence fills the stage. When the curtain rises, the stage is empty. The sound of bells tolling.*

The SERVANT *enters.*

SERVANT. Those bells are making my head ache.

PONCIA (*enters eating bread and sausage*). Two hours and more of all that wailing. Priests have come from all the villages. The church looks lovely. During the first response Magdalena fainted.

SERVANT. She's the one who'll be most alone.

PONCIA. The only one her father loved. Thank God we're alone for a bit. I've come to eat.

SERVANT. If Bernarda sees you!

PONCIA. Now she's not eating, she'd like to see all of us die of hunger! Bossy, domineering creature! She can go to hell! I've opened her sausage-jar!

SERVANT (*sadly, longingly*). Why not give me some for my little girl, Poncia?

PONCIA. In you go. Take a fistful of chickpeas too. She won't be any the wiser today.

VOICE (*off*). Bernarda!

PONCIA. The old woman. Is she locked up properly?

CRIADA. Con dos vueltas de llave.

PONCIA. Pero debes poner también la tranca. Tiene unos dedos como cinco ganzúas.

VOZ. ¡Bernarda!

PONCIA (*a voces*). ¡Ya viene! (*A la* CRIADA.) Limpia bien todo. Si Bernarda no ve relucientes las cosas me arrancará los pocos pelos que me quedan.

CRIADA. ¡Qué mujer!

PONCIA. Tirana de todos los que la rodean. Es capaz de sentarse encima de tu corazón y ver cómo te mueres durante un año sin que se le cierre esa sonrisa fría que lleva en su maldita cara. ¡Limpia, limpia ese vidriado!

CRIADA. Sangre en las manos tengo de fregarlo todo.

PONCIA. Ella la más aseada, ella la más decente, ella la más alta. Buen descanso ganó su pobre marido.

Cesan las campanas.

CRIADA. ¿Han venido todos sus parientes?

PONCIA. Los de ella. La gente de él la odia. Vinieron a verlo muerto, y le hicieron la cruz.

CRIADA. ¿Hay bastantes sillas?

PONCIA. Sobran. Que se sienten en el suelo. Desde que murió el padre de Bernarda no han vuelto a entrar las gentes bajo estos techos. Ella no quiere que la vean en su dominio. ¡Maldita sea!

CRIADA. Contigo se portó bien.

PONCIA. Treinta años lavando sus sábanas, treinta años comiendo sus sobras, noches en vela cuando tose, días enteros mirando por la rendija para espiar a los vecinos y llevarle el cuento; vida sin secretos una con otra, y sin embargo, ¡maldita sea! ¡mal dolor de clavo le pinche en los ojos!

SERVANT. Two turns of the key.

PONCIA. You should put the bar across as well. Her fingers are like five skeleton-keys.

VOICE. Bernarda!

PONCIA (*calling out*). She's coming! (*To the* SERVANT.) Clean everything properly. If Bernarda doesn't see things shining here, she'll pull out what little hair I've still got left.

SERVANT. That woman!

PONCIA. Tyrant of all she surveys. She could sit on your heart and watch you die for a whole year, and that cold smile would still be fixed on her damned face. Now get those dishes clean!

SERVANT. My hands are bleeding from all the washing-up!

PONCIA. She's the cleanest, the most respectable, the most high and mighty. Her poor husband's earned himself a good rest!

The bells stop.

SERVANT. Did all his relatives come?

PONCIA. Only hers. His people hate her. They came to see the corpse and good riddance to him.

SERVANT. Have we got enough chairs?

PONCIA. More than enough. Let them sit on the floor. Since Bernarda's father died, no one has ever set foot in this house. She doesn't want them to see her on her own ground. Damn her!

SERVANT. She's always been good to you.

PONCIA. Thirty years of washing her sheets. Thirty years of eating her scraps. Up all night when she's got a cough. Day in day out spying on the neighbours through the cracks to bring her all the gossip. No secrets between us. But I still say 'Damn her!' I'd like to stick a red-hot nail in her eyes!

CRIADA. ¡Mujer!

PONCIA. Pero yo soy buena perra: ladro cuando me lo dice y muerdo los talones de los que piden limosna cuando ella me azuza; mis hijos trabajan en sus tierras y ya están los dos casados, pero un día me hartaré.

CRIADA. Y ese día . . .

PONCIA. Ese día me encerraré con ella en un cuarto y le estaré escupiendo un año entero: 'Bernarda, por esto, por aquello, por lo otro', hasta ponerla como un lagarto machacado por los niños, que es lo que es ella y toda su parentela. Claro es que no le envidio la vida. Le quedan cinco mujeres, cinco hijas feas, que quitando a Angustias, la mayor, que es la hija del primer marido y tiene dineros, las demás mucha puntilla bordada, muchas camisas de hilo, pero pan y uvas por toda herencia.

CRIADA. ¡Ya quisiera tener yo lo que ellas!

PONCIA. Nosotras tenemos nuestras manos y un hoyo en la tierra de la verdad.

CRIADA. Esa es la única tierra que nos dejan a los que no tenemos nada.

PONCIA (*en la alacena*). Este cristal tiene unas motas.

CRIADA. Ni con el jabón ni con bayeta se le quitan.

Suenan las campanas.

PONCIA. El último responso. Me voy a oírlo. A mí me gusta mucho cómo canta el párroco. En el 'Pater noster' subió, subió, subió la voz que parecía un cántaro llenándose de agua poco a poco. ¡Claro es que al final dio un gallo, pero da gloria oírlo! Ahora que nadie como el antiguo sacristán, Tronchapinos. En la misa de mi madre, que esté en gloria, cantó. Retumbaban las paredes, y cuando decía amén era como si un lobo hubiese entrado en la iglesia. (*Imitándolo.*) ¡Amééééén! (*Se echa a toser.*)

SERVANT. Woman!

PONCIA. But I'm still a good bitch. I bark when I'm told, and when she sets me on them I bite the heels of those who come here looking for charity. My sons work in her fields and both of them are married now, but the day will come when I'll have had enough.

SERVANT. And on that day . . .

PONCIA. On that day I'll lock myself in a room with her and I'll spit on her for a whole year: 'Bernarda, for this, for that, for that other thing', till she looks like a lizard squashed by the kids, which is what she is, and all her family too. Mind you, I don't feel any envy. Five girls still on her hands, five ugly daughters, and only the eldest, Angustias, has any money, since she's the first husband's child. As for the rest, lots of fine lace and lots of linen petticoats, but nothing to inherit but bread and grapes.

SERVANT. If only I could have that!

PONCIA. We've got our hands and a hole in God's earth.

SERVANT. The only land they give to us who have nothing.

PONCIA (*by the cupboard*). This glass has still got marks on it.

SERVANT. They won't come off, not even with soap or rag.

The bells ring out.

PONCIA. The last prayer. I'm going to hear it. I love the way the priest sings! In the paternoster his voice went up and up and up like a pitcher slowly filling with water. It cracked in the end, of course, but it's such a joy to hear him. Even so, there's no one like Tronchapinos, the old sacristan. He sang at the mass for my mother, God rest her soul! The walls used to shake and when he'd get to the Amen, it was as if a wolf had entered the church. (*She imitates him.*) A-a-a-m-m-e-e-n-n! (*She begins to cough.*)

CRIADA. Te vas a hacer el gaznate polvo.

PONCIA. ¡Otra cosa hacía polvo yo! (*Sale riendo.*)

La CRIADA *limpia. Suenan las campanas.*

CRIADA (*llevando el canto*). Tin, tin, tan. Tin, tin, tan. ¡Dios lo haya perdonado!

MENDIGA (*con una niña*). ¡Alabado sea Dios!

CRIADA. Tin, tin, tan. ¡Que nos espere muchos años! Tin, tin, tan.

MENDIGA (*fuerte con cierta irritación*). ¡Alabado sea Dios!

CRIADA (*irritada*). ¡Por siempre!

MENDIGA. Vengo por las sobras.

Cesan las campanas.

CRIADA. Por la puerta se va a la calle. Las sobras de hoy son para mí.

MENDIGA. Mujer, tú tienes quien te gane. Mi niña y yo estamos solas.

CRIADA. También están solos los perros y viven.

MENDIGA. Siempre me las dan.

CRIADA. Fuera de aquí. ¿Quién os dijo que entrarais? Ya me habéis dejado los pies señalados. (*Se van. Limpia.*) Suelos barnizados con aceite, alacenas, pedestales, camas de acero, para que traguemos quina las que vivimos en las chozas de tierra con un plato y una cuchara. ¡Ojalá que un día no quedáramos ni uno para contarlo! (*Vuelven a sonar las campanas.*) Sí, sí, ¡vengan clamores! ¡venga caja con filos dorados y toallas de seda para llevarla!; ¡que lo mismo estarás tú que estaré yo!

SERVANT. You'll strain your windpipe.

PONCIA. I used to strain something else! (*She goes out laughing.*)

The SERVANT *scrubs. The bells ring out.*

SERVANT (*taking up the rhythm*). Ding, dong, ding! Ding, dong, ding! May God forgive him!

BEGGAR WOMAN (*with a little girl*). Praise be to God!

SERVANT. Ding, dong, ding! Let Him wait for us for years to come! Ding, dong, ding!

BEGGAR WOMAN (*loudly, with a certain irritation*). God be praised!

SERVANT (*annoyed*). For ever and ever!

BEGGAR WOMAN. I've come for the scraps.

The bells stop.

SERVANT. That's the way out. Today's scraps are for me!

BEGGAR WOMAN. Woman, you've got someone to look after you. My girl and me, we're on our own.

SERVANT. So are the dogs and they survive.

BEGGAR WOMAN. They always give me them.

SERVANT. Get out of here! Who said you could come in? Look at the mess you've made with your feet!

The BEGGAR WOMAN *leaves. The* SERVANT *scrubs.*

Floors polished with oil, cupboards, pedestals, iron bedsteads. A bitter pill to swallow for those of us who live in huts of mud, with a plate and a spoon. I pray for the day when none of us is left to tell the tale!

The bells begin to peal again.

Yes, come on, bells! Ring out! Bring the wooden box with its fine gold trim and the silk straps to carry it! We'll both end up the same! You can rot, Antonio

Fastídiate, Antonio María Benavides, tieso con tu traje de paño y tus botas enterizas. ¡Fastídiate! ¡Ya no volverás a levantarme las enaguas detrás de la puerta de tu corral!

Por el fondo, de dos en dos, empiezan a entrar MUJERES DE LUTO *con pañuelos, grandes faldas y abanicos negros. Entran lentamente hasta llenar la escena.*

CRIADA (*rompiendo a gritar*). ¡Ay Antonio María Benavides, que ya no verás estas paredes, ni comerás el pan de esta casa! Yo fui la que más te quiso de las que te sirvieron. (*Tirándose del cabello.*) ¿Y he de vivir yo después de haberte marchado? ¿Y he de vivir?

Terminan de entrar las doscientas MUJERES *y aparece* BERNARDA *y sus cinco hijas.* BERNARDA *viene apoyada en un bastón.*

BERNARDA (*a la* CRIADA). ¡Silencio!

CRIADA (*llorando*). ¡Bernarda!

BERNARDA. Menos gritos y más obras. Debías haber procurado que todo esto estuviera más limpio para recibir al duelo. Vete. No es éste tu lugar. (*La* CRIADA *se va sollozando.*) Los pobres son como los animales. Parece como si estuvieran hechos de otras sustancias.

MUJER 1. Los pobres sienten también sus penas.

BERNARDA. Pero las olvidan delante de un plato de garbanzos.

MUCHACHA (*con timidez*). Comer es necesario para vivir.

BERNARDA. A tu edad no se habla delante de las personas mayores.

MUJER 1. Niña, cállate.

BERNARDA. No he dejado que nadie me dé lecciones. Sentarse.

María Benavides, stiff in your woven suit and your high boots! You can rot! Never again will you lift my skirt behind the stable door!

At the back of the stage, two by two, the WOMEN MOURNERS *enter. They wear black skirts and shawls and carry black fans. They enter slowly until the stage is full.*

SERVANT (*begins to wail*). Oh, Antonio María Benavides! Never again will you see these walls or eat the bread of this house! Of all the women who served you, I was the one who loved you most. (*Pulling at her hair.*) Must I go on living after you've gone? Must I go on living?

The two hundred WOMEN *have stopped coming in. Enter* BERNARDA *and her five daughters.* BERNARDA *leans on a stick.*

BERNARDA (*to the* SERVANT). Silence!

SERVANT (*weeping*). Bernarda!

BERNARDA. Less howling and more work! You should have made sure that this was cleaner for the mourners. Get out! This isn't your place.

The SERVANT *goes out in tears.*

The poor are like animals. It's as if they are made of different stuff.

FIRST WOMAN. The poor feel their sorrows too.

BERNARDA. They forget them in front of a plateful of chickpeas.

GIRL (*timidly*). You have to eat to live.

BERNARDA. A girl of your age doesn't speak in front of her elders.

FIRST WOMAN. Child, be quiet!

BERNARDA. I've never let anyone lecture me. Be seated!

Se sientan. Pausa.

(*Fuerte.*) Magdalena, no llores. Si quieres llorar te metes debajo de la cama. ¿Me has oído?

MUJER 2 (*a* BERNARDA). ¿Habéis empezado los trabajos en la era?

BERNARDA. Ayer.

MUJER 3. Cae el sol como plomo.

MUJER 1. Hace años no he conocido calor igual.

Pausa. Se abanican todas.

BERNARDA. ¿Está hecha la limonada?

PONCIA (*sale con una gran bandeja llena de jarritas blancas, que distribuye*). Sí, Bernarda.

BERNARDA. Dale a los hombres.

PONCIA. La están tomando en el patio.

BERNARDA. Que salgan por donde han entrado. No quiero que pasen por aquí.

MUCHACHA (*a* ANGUSTIAS). Pepe el Romano estaba con los hombres del duelo.

ANGUSTIAS. Allí estaba.

BERNARDA. Estaba su madre. Ella ha visto a su madre. A Pepe no lo ha visto ni ella ni yo.

MUCHACHA. Me pareció . . .

BERNARDA. Quien sí estaba era el viudo de Darajalí. Muy cerca de tu tía. A ése lo vimos todas.

MUJER 2 (*aparte y en baja voz*). ¡Mala, más que mala!

MUJER 3 (*aparte y en baja voz*). ¡Lengua de cuchillo!

BERNARDA. Las mujeres en la iglesia no deben mirar más hombre que al oficiante, y a ése porque tiene faldas. Volver la cabeza es buscar el calor de la pana.

They sit. Pause.

(*Strongly.*) Magdalena, stop crying. If you want to cry, get under your bed. Do you hear me?

SECOND WOMAN (*to* BERNARDA). Have you started the threshing?

BERNARDA. Yesterday.

THIRD WOMAN. The sun beats down like lead.

FIRST WOMAN. I haven't known it so hot for years.

Pause. They all fan themselves.

BERNARDA. Is the lemonade ready?

PONCIA. Yes, Bernarda.

She enters with a large tray full of small white jars which she hands out.

BERNARDA. Give some to the men.

PONCIA. They've got some in the courtyard.

BERNARDA. Make sure they leave the way they came in. I don't want them coming through here.

GIRL (*to* ANGUSTIAS). Pepe el Romano was with the mourners.

ANGUSTIAS. Yes, he was.

BERNARDA. His mother was! She saw his mother! Neither of us saw Pepe.

GIRL. I thought . . .

BERNARDA. The one who *was* there was the widower from Darajalí. Very close to your aunt. We all saw him!

SECOND WOMAN (*aside, whispering*). Such a wicked woman! Worse than wicked!

THIRD WOMAN (*aside, whispering*). Tongue like a knife!

BERNARDA. Women in church should look at no other man but the priest – and only at him because he wears skirts. Those who turn their heads are looking for the warmth of a pair of trousers.

MUJER I (*en voz baja.*) ¡Vieja lagarta recocida!

PONCIA (*entre dientes.*) ¡Sarmentosa por calentura de varón!

BERNARDA (*dando un golpe de bastón en el suelo*). Alabado sea Dios.

TODAS (*santiguándose*). Sea por siempre bendito y alabado.

BERNARDA.
Descansa en paz con la santa
compaña de cabecera.

TODAS.
¡Descansa en paz!

BERNARDA.
Con el ángel San Miguel
y su espada justiciera.

TODAS.
¡Descansa en paz!

BERNARDA.
Con la llave que todo lo abre
y la mano que todo lo cierra.

TODAS.
¡Descansa en paz!

BERNARDA.
Con los bienaventurados
y las lucecitas del campo.

TODAS.
¡Descansa en paz!

BERNARDA.
Con nuestra santa caridad
y las almas de tierra y mar.

TODAS.
¡Descansa en paz!

BERNARDA. Concede el reposo a tu siervo Antonio María Benavides y dale la corona de tu santa gloria.

FIRST WOMAN (*whispering*). Dried-up old lizard!

PONCIA (*muttering*). Like a twisted vine reaching out for the heat of a man!

BERNARDA (*beating the floor with her stick*). Praise be to God!

ALL (*crossing themselves*). Blessed and praised for ever!

BERNARDA.

Rest in peace, with the heavenly host
above you.

ALL.

Rest in peace!

BERNARDA.

With the Archangel Saint Michael
and his sword of justice.

ALL.

Rest in peace!

BERNARDA.

With the key that opens all
and the hand that closes all.

ALL.

Rest in peace!

BERNARDA.

With those that are blessed
and the little lights of the field.

ALL.

Rest in peace!

BERNARDA.

With our holy charity
and the souls on land and sea.

ALL.

Rest in peace!

BERNARDA. Grant peace to your servant Antonio María Benavides and give him the crown of your blessed glory!

TODAS. Amén.

BERNARDA (*se pone de pie y canta*). Requiem aeternam dona eis, Domine.

TODAS (*de pie y cantando al modo gregoriano*). Et lux perpetua luceat eis. (*Se santiguan.*)

MUJER I. Salud para rogar por su alma.

> *Van desfilando.*

MUJER 3. No te faltará la hogaza de pan caliente.

MUJER 2. Ni el techo para tus hijas.

> *Van desfilando todas por delante de* BERNARDA *y saliendo. Sale* ANGUSTIAS *por otra puerta, la que da al patio.*

MUJER 4. El mismo lujo de tu casamiento lo sigas disfrutando.

PONCIA (*entrando con una bolsa*). De parte de los hombres esta bolsa de dineros para responsos.

BERNARDA. Dales las gracias y échales una copa de aguardiente.

MUCHACHA (*a* MAGDALENA). Magdalena.

BERNARDA (*a* MAGDALENA, *que inicia el llanto*). Chiss. (*Golpea con el bastón. Salen todas. A las que se han ido.*) ¡Andar a vuestras cuevas a criticar todo lo que habéis visto! Ojalá tardéis muchos años en pasar el arco de mi puerta.

PONCIA. No tendrás queja ninguna. Ha venido todo el pueblo.

BERNARDA. Sí, para llenar mi casa con el sudor de sus refajos y el veneno de sus lenguas.

AMELIA. ¡Madre, no hable usted así!

BERNARDA. Es así como se tiene que hablar en este maldito pueblo sin río, pueblo de pozos, donde siempre

ALL. Amen!

BERNARDA (*getting to her feet, chanting*). *Requiem aeternam dona eis, Domine.*

ALL (*standing and chanting in the Gregorian fashion*). *Et lux perpetua luceat eis.* (*They cross themselves.*)

FIRST WOMAN. God grant you health to pray for his soul.

They are filing out.

THIRD WOMAN. You shall never want for a loaf of bread.

SECOND WOMAN. Nor a roof over your daughters' heads.

They all file out past BERNARDA. ANGUSTIAS *goes out through another door, the one which leads to the courtyard.*

FOURTH WOMAN. May you still enjoy the blessings of your marriage.

PONCIA (*entering with a bag*). From the men. This bag of money for prayers.

BERNARDA. Thank them and pour them a glass of brandy.

GIRL (*to* MAGDALENA). Magdalena . . .

BERNARDA (*to* MAGDALENA, *who is starting to cry*). Sh-h-h!

She bangs with her stick. The WOMEN *go out.*

(*To those who are leaving*). Get back to your caves and criticise all that you've seen! Let it be years before you cross my threshold again!

PONCIA. You can't complain, Bernarda. The whole village came.

BERNARDA. Yes, to fill my house with the sweat of their underskirts and their poisonous tongues!

AMELIA. Mother, don't say that!

BERNARDA. What else can you say of this terrible village without a river . . . this town of wells where we drink

se bebe el agua con el miedo de que esté envenenada.

PONCIA. ¡Cómo han puesto la solería!

BERNARDA. Igual que si hubiera pasado por ella una manada de cabras. (*La* PONCIA *limpia el suelo.*) Niña, dame un abanico.

ADELA. Tome usted. (*Le da un abanico redondo con flores rojas y verdes.*)

BERNARDA (*arrojando el abanico al suelo*). ¿Es éste el abanico que se da a una viuda? Dame uno negro y aprende a respetar el luto de tu padre.

MARTIRIO. Tome usted el mío.

BERNARDA. ¿Y tú?

MARTIRIO. Yo no tengo calor.

BERNARDA. Pues busca otro, que te hará falta. En ocho años que dure el luto no ha de entrar en esta casa el viento de la calle. Haceros cuenta que hemos tapiado con ladrillos puertas y ventanas. Así pasó en casa de mi padre y en casa de mi abuelo. Mientras, podéis empezar a bordaros el ajuar. En el arca tengo veinte piezas de hilo con el que podréis cortar sábanas y embozos. Magdalena puede bordarlas.

MAGDALENA. Lo mismo me da.

ADELA (*agria*). Si no quieres bordarlas irán sin bordados. Así las tuyas lucirán más.

MAGDALENA. Ni las mías ni las vuestras. Sé que yo no me voy a casar. Prefiero llevar sacos al molino. Todo menos estar sentada días y días dentro de esta sala oscura.

BERNARDA. Eso tiene ser mujer.

MAGDALENA. Malditas sean las mujeres.

BERNARDA. Aquí se hace lo que yo mando. Ya no puedes ir con el cuento a tu padre. Hilo y aguja para las hembras. Látigo y mula para el varón. Eso tiene la gente que nace con posibles.

the water and we're always afraid it might be poisoned.

PONCIA. Look what they've done to the floor!

BERNARDA. As if a herd of goats had walked across it!

PONCIA *scrubs the floor.*

Child, give me a fan.

ADELA. Take this one. (*She gives her a round fan decorated with red and green flowers.*)

BERNARDA (*hurling the fan to the floor*). Is this the fan to give a widow? Give me a black one and learn to respect the mourning for your father.

MARTIRIO. Take mine.

BERNARDA. What about you?

MARTIRIO. I don't feel hot.

BERNARDA. Then find another one. You are going to need it. In the eight years this mourning will last the wind from the street shan't enter this house. Imagine we'd sealed the doors and the windows with bricks. That's how it was in my father's house, in my grandfather's too. In the meantime you can start to embroider your trousseaus. I have twenty pieces of linen in the chest for cutting out sheets. Magdalena can embroider them.

MAGDALENA. It's all the same to me.

ADELA (*sharply*). If you don't want to embroider ours, leave them plain! Then yours will look much better.

MAGDALENA. I'd rather not embroider any. I know I'll never get married. I'd rather carry sacks to the mill. Anything but sit here day after day in this dark room.

BERNARDA. That's what it means to be a woman.

MAGDALENA. A curse on women!

BERNARDA. Here you'll do what I say. You can't carry tales to your father now. A needle and thread for women. A whip and a mule for men. That's how it is for people with means.

Sale ADELA.

VOZ. Bernarda, ¡déjame salir!
BERNARDA (*en voz alta*). ¡Dejadla ya!

Sale la CRIADA.

CRIADA. Me ha costado mucho trabajo sujetarla. A pesar
de sus ochenta años tu madre es fuerte como un roble.
BERNARDA. Tiene a quien parecérsele. Mi abuela fue
igual.
CRIADA. Tuve durante el duelo que taparle varias veces la
boca con un costal vacío porque quería llamarte para
que le dieras agua de fregar siquiera, para beber, y carne
de perro, que es lo que ella dice que le das.
MARTIRIO. Tiene mala intención.
BERNARDA (*a la* CRIADA). Déjala que se desahogue en el
patio.
CRIADA. Ha sacado del cofre sus anillos y los pendientes
de amatistas, se los ha puesto y me ha dicho que se
quiere casar.

Las hijas ríen.

BERNARDA. Ve con ella y ten cuidado que no se acerque al
pozo.
CRIADA. No tengas miedo que se tire.
BERNARDA. No es por eso. Pero desde aquel sitio las
vecinas pueden verla desde su ventana.

Sale la CRIADA.

MARTIRIO. Nos vamos a cambiar la ropa.
BERNARDA. Sí, pero no el pañuelo de la cabeza. (*Entra*
ADELA.) ¿Y Angustias?
ADELA (*con retintín*). La he visto asomada a la rendija del

ADELA *goes out.*

VOICE (*off*). Bernarda! Let me out!
BERNARDA (*calling*). Let her out now!

The SERVANT *enters.*

SERVANT. I could hardly hold her. She may be eighty, but your mother's as strong as an oak tree.
BERNARDA. She has someone to live up to. My grand-mother was the same.
SERVANT. Several times, while the mourners were here, I had to cover her mouth with an empty sack. She wanted to call you, so you could give her the dishwater and the dog-meat she says you always give her.
MARTIRIO. She wants to cause trouble.
BERNARDA (*to the* SERVANT). She can let off steam in the courtyard.
SERVANT. She's taken her rings and the amethyst ear-rings from the jewel-box. She's put them on and she says she wants to get married.

The daughters laugh.

BERNARDA. Go with her. Make sure she doesn't go near the well.
SERVANT. Don't worry, she won't throw herself in.
BERNARDA. It's not that – from there the neighbours can see her from their windows.

The SERVANT *goes out.*

MARTIRIO. We're going to change.
BERNARDA. Very well, but not your headscarves.

ADELA *enters.*

Where's Angustias?
ADELA (*pointedly*). I saw her peeping through the crack in

portón. Los hombres se acababan de ir.

BERNARDA. ¿Y tú a qué fuiste también al portón?

ADELA. Me llegué a ver si habían puesto las gallinas.

BERNARDA. ¡Pero el duelo de los hombres habría salido ya!

ADELA (*con intención*). Todavía estaba un grupo parado por fuera.

BERNARDA (*furiosa*). ¡Angustias! ¡Angustias!

ANGUSTIAS (*entrando*). ¿Qué manda usted?

BERNARDA. ¿Qué mirabas y a quién?

ANGUSTIAS. A nadie.

BERNARDA. ¿Es decente que una mujer de tu clase vaya con el anzuelo detrás de un hombre el día de la misa de su padre? ¡Contesta! ¿A quién mirabas?

Pausa.

ANGUSTIAS. Yo . . .

BERNARDA. ¡Tú!

ANGUSTIAS. ¡A nadie!

BERNARDA (*avanzando con el bastón*). ¡Suave! ¡dulzarrona! (*Le da.*)

PONCIA (*corriendo*). ¡Bernarda, cálmate! (*La sujeta.*)

ANGUSTIAS *llora.*

BERNARDA. ¡Fuera de aquí todas!

Salen.

PONCIA. Ella lo ha hecho sin dar alcance a lo que hacía, que está francamente mal. ¡Ya me chocó a mí verla escabullirse hacia el patio! Luego estuvo detrás de una ventana oyendo la conversación que traían los hombres, que como siempre no se puede oír.

BERNARDA. ¡A eso vienen a los duelos! (*Con curiosidad.*) ¿De qué hablaban?

the main door. The men had just left.

BERNARDA. And why were you at the door?

ADELA. I went to see if the hens had laid.

BERNARDA. But the men must have left already.

ADELA (*pointedly*). There was still a group standing outside.

BERNARDA (*furiously*). Angustias! Angustias!

ANGUSTIAS (*entering*). What is it?

BERNARDA. What were you looking at? And who?

ANGUSTIAS. No one.

BERNARDA. Is it proper for a woman of your class to be throwing a man the bait on the day of her father's funeral? Answer me! Who were you looking at?

Pause.

ANGUSTIAS. I . . .

BERNARDA. Yes, you.

ANGUSTIAS. No one.

BERNARDA (*advancing with her stick*). You soft, smarmy creature! (*She strikes her.*)

PONCIA (*running*). Bernarda! Calm yourself! (*She holds her.*)

ANGUSTIAS *is crying.*

BERNARDA. Get out, all of you!

They leave.

PONCIA. She did it without thinking. It was wrong, of course. It gave me quite a shock to see her sneaking towards the courtyard. Then she stood by a window, listening to the men's conversation. As usual, it was disgusting.

BERNARDA. And they come to funerals for that! (*With curiosity.*) What were they talking about?

PONCIA. Hablaban de Paca la Roseta. Anoche ataron a su marido a un pesebre y a ella se la llevaron a la grupa del caballo hasta lo alto del olivar.

BERNARDA. ¿Y ella?

PONCIA. Ella tan conforme. Dicen que iba con los pechos fuera y Maximiliano la llevaba cogida como si tocara la guitarra. ¡Un horror!

BERNARDA. ¿Y qué pasó?

PONCIA. Lo que tenía que pasar. Volvieron casi de día. Paca la Roseta traía el pelo suelto y una corona de flores en la cabeza.

BERNARDA. Es la única mujer mala que tenemos en el pueblo.

PONCIA. Porque no es de aquí. Es de muy lejos. Y los que fueron con ella son también hijos de forastero. Los hombres de aquí no son capaces de eso.

BERNARDA. No, pero les gusta verlo y comentarlo, y se chupan los dedos de que esto ocurra.

PONCIA. Contaban muchas cosas más.

BERNARDA (*mirando a un lado y otro con cierto temor*). ¿Cuáles?

PONCIA. Me da vergüenza referirlas.

BERNARDA. Y mi hija las oyó.

PONCIA. ¡Claro!

BERNARDA. Esa sale a sus tías; blancas y untuosas que ponían ojos de carnero al piropo de cualquier barberillo. ¡Cuánto hay que sufrir y luchar para hacer que las personas sean decentes y no tiren al monte demasiado!

PONCIA. ¡Es que tus hijas están ya en edad de merecer! Demasiada poca guerra te dan. Angustias ya debe tener mucho más de los treinta.

BERNARDA. Treinta y nueve justos.

PONCIA. Figúrate. Y no ha tenido nunca novio...

BERNARDA (*furiosa*). ¡No, no ha tenido novio ninguna, ni les hace falta! Pueden pasarse muy bien.

PONCIA. They were talking about Paca la Roseta. Last night they tied her husband to a trough and carried her off on horseback to the top of the olive-grove.

BERNARDA. What about her?

PONCIA. She was willing. They say she went with her breasts exposed and Maximiliano was holding her tight, as though he was playing the guitar. Disgusting!

BERNARDA. What happened then?

PONCIA. What was bound to happen. They came back when it was almost light. Paca la Roseta had her hair down and a crown of flowers on her head.

BERNARDA. She's the only loose woman in the village.

PONCIA. Because she's not from here. She's from far away. And the men who went with her are the sons of outsiders too. The men here aren't capable of that.

BERNARDA. No, but they like to see it and talk about it and suck their fingers when it happens.

PONCIA. They were saying lots of other things too.

BERNARDA (*looking in all directions with a certain apprehension*). What sort of things?

PONCIA. I'm ashamed to mention them.

BERNARDA. And my daughter heard them!

PONCIA. Of course!

BERNARDA. That one takes after her aunts: white and sugary, and making sheep's eyes at any common barber's flattery. Oh, how we have to suffer and struggle to make sure people behave decently and don't run wild!

PONCIA. The fact is your daughters are old enough to be attractive to men. They give you little enough trouble. Angustias must be well over thirty now.

BERNARDA. Thirty-nine, to be exact.

PONCIA. Imagine! And she's never had a suitor.

BERNARDA (*furiously*). None of them has had a suitor, nor do they need one! They manage as they are!

PONCIA. No he querido ofenderte.

BERNARDA. No hay en cien leguas a la redonda quien se pueda acercar a ellas. Los hombres de aquí no son de su clase. ¿Es que quieres que las entregue a cualquier gañán?

PONCIA. Debías haberte ido a otro pueblo.

BERNARDA. Eso, ¡a venderlas!

PONCIA. No, Bernarda, a cambiar . . . ¡Claro que en otros sitios ellas resultan las pobres!

BERNARDA. ¡Calla esa lengua atormentadora!

PONCIA. Contigo no se puede hablar. ¿Tenemos o no tenemos confianza?

BERNARDA. No tenemos. Me sirves y te pago. ¡Nada más!

CRIADA (entrando). Ahí está don Arturo, que viene a arreglar las particiones.

BERNARDA. Vamos. (A la CRIADA.) Tú empieza a blanquear el patio. (A la PONCIA.) Y tú ve guardando en el arca grande toda la ropa del muerto.

PONCIA. Algunas cosas las podríamos dar . . .

BERNARDA. Nada. ¡Ni un botón! ¡Ni el pañuelo con que le hemos tapado la cara!

> Sale lentamente apoyada en el bastón y al salir vuelve la cabeza y mira a sus CRIADAS. Las CRIADAS salen después. Entran AMELIA y MARTIRIO.

AMELIA. ¿Has tomado la medicina?

MARTIRIO. ¡Para lo que me va a servir!

AMELIA. Pero la has tomado.

MARTIRIO. Ya hago las cosas sin fe, pero como un reloj.

AMELIA. Desde que vino el médico nuevo estás más animada.

MARTIRIO. Yo me siento lo mismo.

AMELIA. ¿Te fijaste? Adelaida no estuvo en el duelo.

MARTIRIO. Ya lo sabía. Su novio no la deja salir ni al

PONCIA. I didn't mean to offend you.

BERNARDA. There's no one for a hundred miles around can match them. The men here at not of their class. Would you have me offer them to some farmhand?

PONCIA. You should have gone to another village.

BERNARDA. Oh, yes! And sold them!

PONCIA. No, Bernarda . . . for a change . . . Somewhere else, of course, they would have been the poor ones.

BERNARDA. Hold your poisonous tongue!

PONCIA. There's no talking to you! Are we old friends or not?

BERNARDA. We are not! You serve me and I pay you. Nothing more!

SERVANT (*entering*). Don Arturo's here to discuss the will.

BERNARDA. All right. (*To the* SERVANT.) You start whitewashing the courtyard walls. (*To* PONCIA.) And you put all the deceased's clothes in the big chest.

PONCIA. We could give some of the things . . .

BERNARDA. Not a thing! Not a button! Not even the handkerchief we used to cover his face!

> *She goes out slowly, leaning on the stick. As she goes, she looks back at her* SERVANTS. *The* SERVANTS *leave too.* AMELIA *and* MARTIRIO *enter.*

AMELIA. Have you taken your medicine?

MARTIRIO. For all the good it'll do me.

AMELIA. But you have taken it?

MARTIRIO. I do things without belief, without thinking.

AMELIA. Since the new doctor came, you've livened up.

MARTIRIO. I feel the same.

AMELIA. Did you notice? Adelaida wasn't at the funeral.

MARTIRIO. I knew she wouldn't be. Her fiancé won't let

tranco de la calle. Antes era alegre; ahora ni polvos se echa en la cara.

AMELIA. Ya no sabe una si es mejor tener novio o no.

MARTIRIO. Es lo mismo.

AMELIA. De todo tiene la culpa esta crítica que no nos deja vivir. Adelaida habrá pasado mal rato.

MARTIRIO. Le tienen miedo a nuestra madre. Es la única que conoce la historia de su padre y el origen de sus tierras. Siempre que viene le tira puñaladas con el asunto. Su padre mató en Cuba al marido de su primera mujer para casarse con ella, luego aquí la abandonó y se fue con otra que tenía una hija, y luego tuvo relaciones con esta muchacha, la madre de Adelaida, y casó con ella después de haber muerto loca la segunda mujer.

AMELIA. Y ese infame, ¿por qué no está en la cárcel?

MARTIRIO. Porque los hombres se tapan unos a otros las cosas de esta índole y nadie es capaz de delatar.

AMELIA. Pero Adelaida no tiene culpa de esto.

MARTIRIO. No, pero las cosas se repiten. Yo veo que todo es una terrible repetición. Y ella tiene el mismo sino de su madre y de su abuela, mujeres las dos del que la engendró.

AMELIA. ¡Qué cosa más grande!

MARTIRIO. Es preferible no ver a un hombre nunca. Desde niña les tuve miedo. Los veía en el corral uncir los bueyes y levantar los costales de trigo entre voces y zapatazos, y siempre tuve miedo de crecer por temor de encontrarme de pronto abrazada por ellos. Dios me ha hecho débil y fea y los ha apartado definitivamente de mí.

AMELIA. ¡Eso no digas! Enrique Humanes estuvo detrás de ti y le gustabas.

MARTIRIO. ¡Invenciones de la gente! Una vez estuve en

her out of the house. She used to be happy. Now she doesn't even powder her face.

AMELIA. It's hard to know any more if you're better off with a suitor or not.

MARTIRIO. It's all the same.

AMELIA. This gossip is to blame, you just can't live with it. Adelaida must have had a bad time.

MARTIRIO. They're terrified of our mother. She's the only one who knows the truth about her father and how he got his land. Whenever she comes here, Mother sticks the knife right in. In Cuba her father killed his first wife's husband in order to marry her. Then, over here, he left her and went off with another woman who had a daughter, and he had an affair with the girl, Adelaida's mother, and he married her after his second wife had gone mad and died.

AMELIA. Why isn't the wicked man in jail?

MARTIRIO. Because men cover up for each other in things like that, and no one's willing to speak out.

AMELIA. But Adelaida's not to blame for that.

MARTIRIO. No, but things repeat themselves. I can see that everything's a terrible repetition. Her fate is the same as her mother's and her grandmother's, both wives to the man who fathered her.

AMELIA. What a terrible thing!

MARTIRIO. Better never to look at a man! I've been afraid of them since I was small. I used to see them in the stable-yard, yoking the oxen and lifting the sacks of wheat, and all of them shouting and stamping their feet. I was always afraid to grow up in case I'd find myself suddenly grabbed by them. God has made me weak and ugly and kept them away from me for ever.

AMELIA. Don't say that! Enrique Humanes was sweet on you once. He liked you.

MARTIRIO. The stories people invent! I waited at my

camisa detrás de la ventana hasta que fue de día, porque me avisó con la hija de su gañán que iba a venir, y no vino. Fue todo cosa de lenguas. Luego se casó con otra que tenía más que yo.

AMELIA. ¡Y fea como un demonio!

MARTIRIO. ¡Qué les importa a ellos la fealdad! A ellos les importa la tierra, las yuntas y una perra sumisa que les dé de comer.

AMELIA. ¡Ay!

Entra MAGDALENA.

MAGDALENA. ¿Qué hacéis?

MARTIRIO. Aquí.

AMELIA. ¿Y tú?

MAGDALENA. Vengo de correr las cámaras. Por andar un poco. De ver los cuadros bordados en cañamazo de nuestra abuela, el perrito de lanas y el negro luchando con el león, que tanto nos gustaba de niñas. Aquélla era una época más alegre. Una boda duraba diez días y no se usaban las malas lenguas. Hoy hay más finura. Las novias se ponen velo blanco como en las poblaciones, y se bebe vino de botella, pero nos pudrimos por el qué dirán.

MARTIRIO. ¡Sabe Dios lo que entonces pasaría!

AMELIA (*a* MAGDALENA). Llevas desabrochados los cordones de un zapato.

MAGDALENA. ¡Qué más da!

AMELIA. ¡Te los vas a pisar y te vas a caer!

MAGDALENA. ¡Una menos!

MARTIRIO. ¿Y Adela?

MAGDALENA. ¡Ah! Se ha puesto el traje verde que se hizo para estrenar el día de su cumpleaños, se ha ido al corral y ha comenzado a voces: '¡Gallinas, gallinas, miradme!' ¡Me he tenido que reír!

AMELIA. ¡Si la hubiera visto madre!

window once in my nightdress till daylight. He'd told his farmhand's daughter to tell me he'd be coming. He never did. It was all just talk. Then he married another girl who had more money.

AMELIA. And as ugly as sin.

MARTIRIO. What's ugliness to them? All they want is land, oxen, and an obedient bitch to feed them.

AMELIA. Ohhh!

MAGDALENA *enters.*

MAGDALENA. What are you doing?

MARTIRIO. Nothing much.

AMELIA. And you?

MAGDALENA. Just walking through the rooms. To stretch my legs. I've been looking at the pictures Grandmother used to embroider on canvas – the little poodle, the black man fighting the lion – the one we liked so much when we were small. That was a happier time. A wedding used to last ten days and spiteful gossip wasn't the fashion. Today there's more refinement, brides wear white veils like they do in the towns, we drink bottled wine, but we waste away for fear of what people might say.

MARTIRIO. God knows what went on in those days!

AMELIA (*to* MAGDALENA). Your shoelace is undone.

MAGDALENA. It doesn't matter!

AMELIA. You'll step on it and fall!

MAGDALENA. One less.

MARTIRIO. Where's Adela?

MAGDALENA. Ah! She put on the green dress that was made to wear on her birthday. She went to the stable-yard and started calling out: 'Hens, hens, look at me.' I had to laugh.

AMELIA. If Mother had seen her!

MAGDALENA. ¡Pobrecilla! Es la más joven de nosotras y tiene ilusión. ¡Daría algo por verla feliz!

Pausa. ANGUSTIAS *cruza la escena con unas toallas en la mano.*

ANGUSTIAS. ¿Qué hora es?
MARTIRIO. Ya deben ser las doce.
ANGUSTIAS. ¿Tanto?
AMELIA. Estarán al caer.

Sale ANGUSTIAS.

MAGDALENA (*con intención.*) ¿Sabéis ya la cosa? ... (*Señalando a* ANGUSTIAS.)
AMELIA. No.
MAGDALENA. ¡Vamos!
MARTIRIO. ¡No sé a qué cosa te refieres! ...
MAGDALENA. Mejor que yo lo sabéis las dos, siempre cabeza con cabeza como dos ovejitas, pero sin desahogaros con nadie. ¡Lo de Pepe el Romano!
MARTIRIO. ¡Ah!
MAGDALENA (*remedándola*). ¡Ah! Ya se comenta por el pueblo. Pepe el Romano viene a casarse con Angustias. Anoche estuvo rondando la casa y creo que pronto va a mandar un emisario.
MARTIRIO. ¡Yo me alegro! Es buen hombre.
AMELIA. Yo también. Angustias tiene buenas condiciones.
MAGDALENA. Ninguna de las dos os alegráis.
MARTIRIO. ¡Magdalena! ¡Mujer!
MAGDALENA. Si viniera por el tipo de Angustias, por Angustias como mujer, yo me alegraría, pero viene por el dinero. Aunque Angustias es nuestra hermana aquí estamos en familia y reconocemos que está vieja, enfermiza, y que siempre ha sido la que ha tenido menos mérito de todas nosotras, porque si con veinte

MAGDALENA. Poor child! The youngest of us all and full of hope. I'd give a lot to see her happy!

Pause. ANGUSTIAS *crosses the stage carrying some towels.*

ANGUSTIAS. What time is it?
MAGDALENA. It must be twelve.
ANGUSTIAS. That late?
AMELIA. It's about to strike.

ANGUSTIAS *leaves.*

MAGDALENA (*pointedly*). Have you heard the news? (*Indicating* ANGUSTIAS.)
AMELIA. No.
MAGDALENA. Come on!
MARTIRIO. I don't know what you mean!
MAGDALENA. Both of you know more than me. Your heads are always together, like two little sheep, but you never confide in anyone else. This business with Pepe el Romano.
MARTIRIO. Ah!
MAGDALENA (*imitating her*). Ah! It's already the talk of the town. Pepe el Romano is to marry Angustias. He was outside the house last night. I think he'll soon be sending someone to ask for her hand.
MARTIRIO. I'm glad. He's a good man.
AMELIA. Me too. Angustias has fine qualities.
MAGDALENA. Neither of you is glad!
MARTIRIO. Magdalena!
MAGDALENA. If he wanted Angustias for her looks, Angustias as a woman, I would be glad. But he's after her money. Even though Angustias is our sister, we're all family here and we know that she's old, sickly, and has always been the one with less to offer than the rest of us.

años parecía un palo vestido, ¡qué será ahora que tiene cuarenta!

MARTIRIO. No hables así. La suerte viene a quien menos la aguarda.

AMELIA. ¡Después de todo dice la verdad! Angustias tiene el dinero de su padre, es la única rica de la casa y por eso ahora, que nuestro padre ha muerto y ya se harán particiones, vienen por ella.

MAGDALENA. Pepe el Romano tiene veinticinco años y es el mejor tipo de todos estos contornos. Lo natural sería que te pretendiera a ti, Amelia, o a nuestra Adela, que tiene veinte años, pero no que venga a buscar lo más oscuro de esta casa, a una mujer que como su padre habla con la nariz.

MARTIRIO. ¡Puede que a él le guste!

MAGDALENA. ¡Nunca he podido resistir tu hipocresía!

MARTIRIO. ¡Dios nos valga!

Entra ADELA.

MAGDALENA. ¿Te han visto ya las gallinas?

ADELA. ¿Y qué querías que hiciera?

AMELIA. ¡Si te ve nuestra madre te arrastra del pelo!

ADELA. Tenía mucha ilusión con el vestido. Pensaba ponérmelo el día que vamos a comer sandías a la noria. No hubiera habido otro igual.

MARTIRIO. ¡Es un vestido precioso!

ADELA. Y me está muy bien. Es lo que mejor ha cortado Magdalena.

MAGDALENA. ¿Y las gallinas qué te han dicho?

ADELA. Regalarme unas cuantas pulgas que me han acribillado las piernas.

Ríen.

If she looked like a stick wrapped in a dress at twenty, what's she like now at forty?

MARTIRIO. Don't talk like that! Luck comes to the one who least expects it.

AMELIA. But she's right! Angustias has her father's money, she's the only rich one in the house, and so, now that our father's dead and his estate is being shared out, they're after her.

MAGDALENA. Pepe el Romano's twenty-five and the best-looking man for miles around. It would be natural if he were courting you, Amelia, or Adela, since she's only twenty. But not to go after the dullest thing in the house, a woman who talks through her nose, just like her father did.

MARTIRIO. Perhaps he likes her!

MAGDALENA. I could never stomach your hypocrisy!

MARTIRIO. Heaven preserve us!

ADELA *enters.*

MAGDALENA. Have the hens seen you yet?

ADELA. What was I supposed to do?

AMELIA. If Mother sees you, she'll drag you by your hair!

ADELA. I was so thrilled with the dress! I was planning to wear it the day we go to eat watermelons by the waterwheel. There wouldn't have been another one like it.

MARTIRIO. It's a lovely dress.

ADELA. And it suits me perfectly. It's the best thing Magdalena's ever made.

MAGDALENA. What did the hens have to say to you?

ADELA. They gave me some of their fleas. My legs are covered in bites.

They laugh.

MARTIRIO. Lo que puedes hacer es teñirlo de negro.

MAGDALENA. ¡Lo mejor que puede hacer es regalárselo a Angustias para su boda con Pepe el Romano!

ADELA (*con emoción contenida*). ¡Pero Pepe el Romano . . . !

AMELIA. ¿No lo has oído decir?

ADELA. No.

MAGDALENA. ¡Pues ya lo sabes!

ADELA. ¡Pero si no puede ser!

MAGDALENA. ¡El dinero lo puede todo!

ADELA. ¿Por eso ha salido detrás del duelo y estuvo mirando por el portón? (*Pausa.*) Y ese hombre es capaz de . . .

MAGDALENA. Es capaz de todo.

Pausa.

MARTIRIO. ¿Qué piensas, Adela?

ADELA. Pienso que este luto me ha cogido en la peor época de mi vida para pasarlo.

MAGDALENA. Ya te acostumbrarás.

ADELA (*rompiendo a llorar con ira*). ¡No, no me acostumbraré! Yo no quiero estar encerrada. No quiero que se me pongan las carnes como a vosotras. ¡No quiero perder mi blancura en estas habitaciones! ¡Mañana me pondré mi vestido verde y me echaré a pasear por la calle! ¡Yo quiero salir!

Entra la CRIADA.

MAGDALENA (*autoritaria*). ¡Adela!

CRIADA. ¡La pobre! ¡Cuánto ha sentido a su padre! (*Sale.*)

MARTIRIO. ¡Calla!

AMELIA. Lo que sea de una será de todas.

ADELA *se calma.*

MARTIRIO. What you can do is dye it black.

MAGDALENA. The best thing she can do is give it to Angustias for her wedding to Pepe el Romano!

ADELA (*with contained emotion*). But Pepe el Romano . . .

AMELIA. Haven't you heard?

ADELA. No.

MAGDALENA. Well now you know!

ADELA. It isn't possible!

MAGDALENA. Money makes everything possible!

ADELA. Is that why she followed the mourners out and looked through the door? (*Pause.*) How could that man . . . ?

MAGDALENA. He's capable of anything.

Pause.

MARTIRIO. What are you thinking, Adela?

ADELA. I think this period of mourning has come at the worst time in my life for me to put up with it.

MAGDALENA. You'll soon get used to it.

ADELA (*bursting into tears of anger*). No, I shan't get used to it! I don't want to be shut away! I don't want my skin to become like yours. I don't want to lose my whiteness in these rooms! Tomorrow I'll put on my green dress and I'll go for a walk down the street! I want to go out!

The SERVANT *appears.*

MAGDALENA (*with authority*). Adela!

SERVANT. The poor child! She misses her father so much! (*She goes out.*)

MARTIRIO. Be quiet!

AMELIA. What will be for one will be for all.

ADELA *calms down.*

MAGDALENA. Ha estado a punto de oírte la criada.

CRIADA (*apareciendo*). Pepe el Romano viene por lo alto de la calle.

AMELIA, MARTIRIO y MAGDALENA *corren presurosas*.

MAGDALENA. ¡Vamos a verlo!

Salen rápidas.

CRIADA (*a* ADELA). ¿Tú no vas?

ADELA. No me importa.

CRIADA. Como dará la vuelta a la esquina, desde la ventana de tu cuarto se verá mejor. (*Sale la* CRIADA.)

ADELA *queda en escena dudando. Después de un instante se va también rápida hacia su habitación. Salen* BERNARDA *y la* PONCIA.

BERNARDA. ¡Malditas particiones!

PONCIA. ¡Cuánto dinero le queda a Angustias!

BERNARDA. Sí.

PONCIA. Y a las otras bastante menos.

BERNARDA. Ya me lo has dicho tres veces y no te he querido replicar. Bastante menos, mucho menos. No me lo recuerdes más.

Sale ANGUSTIAS *muy compuesta de cara.*

¡Angustias!

ANGUSTIAS. Madre.

BERNARDA. ¿Pero has tenido valor de echarte polvos en la cara? ¿Has tenido valor de lavarte la cara el día de la misa de tu padre?

ANGUSTIAS. No era mi padre. El mío murió hace tiempo. ¿Es que ya no lo recuerda usted?

BERNARDA. ¡Más debes a este hombre, padre de tus hermanas, que al tuyo! Gracias a este hombre tienes

MAGDALENA. The servant almost heard you.

SERVANT (*entering*). Pepe el Romano's at the top of the street.

AMELIA, MARTIRIO *and* MAGDALENA *run quickly.*

MAGDALENA. Let's go and see him!

They run out.

SERVANT (*to* ADELA). Aren't you going?

ADELA. I'm not bothered.

SERVANT. When he turns the corner, you can see him better from the window of your room. (*The* SERVANT *leaves.*)

ADELA *hesitates. After a moment she also rushes out to her room.* BERNARDA *and* PONCIA *enter.*

BERNARDA. Damn the will!

PONCIA. Such a lot of money for Angustias!

BERNARDA. Yes.

PONCIA. And for the others quite a lot less!

BERNARDA. You've told me that three times already and I chose not to answer you. Quite a lot less, much less. Don't remind me again.

ANGUSTIAS *enters, her face heavily made-up.*

Angustias!

ANGUSTIAS. Mother?

BERNARDA. How dare you powder your face! How dare you wash your face on the day of your father's funeral!

ANGUSTIAS. He wasn't my father. Mine died a long time ago. Don't you remember him any more?

BERNARDA. You owe this man, your sisters' father, more than your own! Thanks to this man you have a fortune.

colmada tu fortuna.

ANGUSTIAS. ¡Eso lo teníamos que ver!

BERNARDA. ¡Aunque fuera por decencia! Por respeto.

ANGUSTIAS. Madre, déjeme usted salir.

BERNARDA. ¿Salir? Después que te haya quitado esos polvos de la cara. ¡Suavona! ¡yeyo! ¡espejo de tus tías! (*Le quita violentamente con su pañuelo los polvos.*) ¡Ahora vete!

PONCIA. ¡Bernarda, no seas tan inquisitiva!

BERNARDA. Aunque mi madre esté loca yo estoy con mis cinco sentidos y sé perfectamente lo que hago.

Entran todas.

MAGDALENA. ¿Qué pasa?

BERNARDA. No pasa nada.

MAGDALENA (*a* ANGUSTIAS). Si es que discutís por las particiones, tú, que eres la más rica, te puedes quedar con todo.

ANGUSTIAS. ¡Guárdate la lengua en la madriguera!

BERNARDA (*golpeando con el bastón en el suelo*). ¡No os hagáis ilusiones de que vais a poder conmigo! ¡Hasta que salga de esta casa con los pies adelante mandaré en lo mío y en lo vuestro!

Se oyen unas voces y entra en escena MARÍA JOSEFA, *la madre de* BERNARDA, *viejísima, ataviada con flores en la cabeza y en el pecho.*

MARÍA JOSEFA. Bernarda, ¿dónde está mi mantilla? Nada de lo que tengo quiero que sea para vosotras, ni mis anillos, ni mi traje negro de moaré, porque ninguna de vosotras se va a casar. ¡Ninguna! ¡Bernarda, dame mi gargantilla de perlas!

BERNARDA (*a la* CRIADA). ¿Por qué la habéis dejado entrar?

ANGUSTIAS. That remains to be seen.

BERNARDA. If only for decency's sake! Out of respect!

ANGUSTIAS. Mother, let me go out!

BERNARDA. Go out? After I've scrubbed that powder from your face. You two-faced creature! Painted doll! The image of your aunts! (*With a handkerchief she forcefully wipes the powder from her face.*) Now get out!

PONCIA. Bernarda, don't be so hard!

BERNARDA. My mother may be mad, but I've still got all my faculties. I know exactly what I'm doing.

The other daughters enter.

MAGDALENA. What's going on?

BERNARDA. Nothing's going on.

MAGDALENA (*to* ANGUSTIAS). If you're arguing about the inheritance, you are the richest anyway, you can keep it all.

ANGUSTIAS. You keep your tongue where it belongs!

BERNARDA (*banging the floor with her stick*). Don't you imagine you can get the better of me. Until I leave this house feet first, I shall control my own affairs and yours!

Voices are heard and MARÍA JOSEFA, BERNARDA's *mother, appears, very old and decked out with flowers in her hair and at her bosom.*

MARÍA JOSEFA. Bernarda where's my mantilla? I want none of my things to be yours. Not my rings nor my black moiré dress. Because none of you will get married. Not one! Bernarda, give me my pearl necklace!

BERNARDA (*to the* SERVANT). Why did you let her in here?

CRIADA (*temblando*). ¡Se me escapó!

MARÍA JOSEFA. Me escapé porque me quiero casar, porque quiero casarme con un varón hermoso de la orilla del mar, ya que aquí los hombres huyen de las mujeres.

BERNARDA. ¡Calle usted, madre!

MARÍA JOSEFA. No, no callo. No quiero ver a estas mujeres solteras, rabiando por la boda, haciéndose polvo el corazón, y yo me quiero ir a mi pueblo. ¡Bernarda, yo quiero un varón para casarme y tener alegría!

BERNARDA. ¡Encerradla!

MARÍA JOSEFA. Déjame salir, Bernarda.

La CRIADA *coge a* MARÍA JOSEFA.

BERNARDA. ¡Ayudarla vosotras!

Todas arrastran a la vieja.

MARÍA JOSEFA. ¡Quiero irme de aquí! ¡Bernarda! A casarme a la orilla del mar, a la orilla del mar.

Telón rápido.

SERVANT (*trembling*). She got away from me.

MARÍA JOSEFA. I escaped because I want to get married, because I want to marry a beautiful man from the seashore. Because the men here run away from women.

BERNARDA. Be quiet, Mother!

MARÍA JOSEFA. I won't be quiet! I don't want to see these spinster women, aching for marriage, eating their hearts out, and I want to go back to my village. Bernarda, I want a man to marry and be happy!

BERNARDA. Lock her up!

MARÍA JOSEFA. Let me go out, Bernarda!

The SERVANT *takes hold of* MARÍA JOSEFA.

BERNARDA. Help her, all of you!

They drag the old woman away.

MARÍA JOSEFA. I want to leave here, Bernarda! To get married on the seashore, on the seashore.

Quick curtain.

Acto Segundo

Habitación blanca del interior de la casa de BERNARDA.
*Las puertas de la izquierda dan a los dormitorios. Las hijas
de* BERNARDA *están sentadas en sillas bajas, cosiendo.*
MAGDALENA *borda. Con ellas está la* PONCIA.

ANGUSTIAS. Ya he cortado la tercera sábana.

MARTIRIO. Le corresponde a Amelia.

MAGDALENA. Angustias, ¿pongo también las iniciales de
Pepe?

ANGUSTIAS (*seca*). No.

MAGDALENA (*a voces*). Adela, ¿no vienes?

AMELIA. Estará echada en la cama.

PONCIA. Esa tiene algo. La encuentro sin sosiego, tem-
blona, asustada como si tuviera una lagartija entre los
pechos.

MARTIRIO. No tiene ni más ni menos que lo que tenemos
todas.

MAGDALENA. Todas menos Angustias.

ANGUSTIAS. Yo me encuentro bien, y al que le duela que
reviente.

MAGDALENA. Desde luego hay que reconocer que lo mejor
que has tenido siempre ha sido el talle y la delicadeza.

ANGUSTIAS. Afortunadamente pronto voy a salir de este
infierno.

MAGDALENA. ¡A lo mejor no sales!

MARTIRIO. ¡Dejar esa conversación!

ANGUSTIAS. Y, además, ¡más vale onza en el arca que ojos
negros en la cara!

MAGDALENA. Por un oído me entra y por otro me sale.

AMELIA (*a la* PONCIA). Abre la puerta del patio a ver si
nos entra un poco el fresco. (*La* PONCIA *lo hace.*)

Act Two

A white inner room in BERNARDA'*s house. The doors on the left lead to the bedrooms.* BERNARDA'*s daughters are sitting on low chairs, sewing.* MAGDALENA *embroiders.* PONCIA *is with them.*

ANGUSTIAS. I've finished cutting the third sheet.

MARTIRIO. It's for Amelia.

MAGDALENA. Angustias, shall I put Pepe's initials too?

ANGUSTIAS (*curtly*). No.

MAGDALENA (*calling out*). Adela, aren't you coming?

AMELIA. She'll be lying on her bed.

PONCIA. There's something wrong with that one. She's restless, all of a tremble, scared, as if she had a lizard between her breasts.

MARTIRIO. There's nothing wrong with her that isn't wrong with all of us.

MAGDALENA. All except Angustias.

ANGUSTIAS. I feel fine, and anyone who doesn't like it can go to hell!

MAGDALENA. Well, one has to admit that the best things about you have always been your figure and your sensitivity.

ANGUSTIAS. Fortunately, I'll soon be out of this hell.

MAGDALENA. Maybe you won't!

MARTIRIO. Let's talk about something else.

ANGUSTIAS. Besides, gold in the coffers is worth more than dark eyes in a pretty face.

MAGDALENA. With me it's in one ear and out the other.

AMELIA (*to* PONCIA). Open the door to the courtyard. Let's get some fresh air in here.

PONCIA *does it.*

MARTIRIO. Esta noche pasada no me podía quedar dormida del calor.

AMELIA. ¡Yo tampoco!

MAGDALENA. Yo me levanté a refrescarme. Había un nublo negro de tormenta y hasta cayeron algunas gotas.

PONCIA. Era la una de la madrugada y salía fuego de la tierra. También me levanté yo. Todavía estaba Angustias con Pepe en la ventana.

MAGDALENA (*con ironía*). ¿Tan tarde? ¿A qué hora se fue?

ANGUSTIAS. Magdalena, ¿a qué preguntas si lo viste?

AMELIA. Se iría a eso de la una y media.

ANGUSTIAS. Sí. ¿Tú por qué lo sabes?

AMELIA. Lo sentí toser y oí los pasos de su jaca.

PONCIA. ¡Pero si yo lo sentí marchar a eso de las cuatro!

ANGUSTIAS. ¡No sería él!

PONCIA. ¡Estoy segura!

AMELIA. A mí también me pareció.

MAGDALENA. ¡Qué cosa más rara!

Pausa.

PONCIA. Oye, Angustias, ¿qué fue lo que te dijo la primera vez que se acercó a tu ventana?

ANGUSTIAS. Nada. ¡Qué me iba a decir! Cosas de conversación.

MARTIRIO. Verdaderamente es raro que dos personas que no se conocen se vean de pronto en una reja y ya novios.

ANGUSTIAS. Pues a mí no me chocó.

AMELIA. A mí me daría no sé qué.

ANGUSTIAS. No, porque cuando un hombre se acerca a una reja ya sabe por los que van y vienen, llevan y traen, que se le va a decir que sí.

MARTIRIO. Bueno, pero él te lo tendría que decir.

MARTIRIO. Last night I couldn't get to sleep at all, it was so hot.

AMELIA. Neither could I.

MAGDALENA. I got up to cool myself off. There was a black storm-cloud and even a few drops of rain.

PONCIA. It was one in the morning and fire was coming out of the ground. I got up too. Angustias was still with Pepe at the window.

MAGDALENA (*with irony*). So late? What time did he leave?

ANGUSTIAS. Magdalena, why ask if you saw him?

AMELIA. He must have left around half-past one.

ANGUSTIAS. Yes. How do *you* know?

AMELIA. I heard him cough and I heard the sound of his mare's hooves.

PONCIA. But I heard him leave around four!

ANGUSTIAS. It wouldn't have been him!

PONCIA. I'm positive!

AMELIA. I thought so too.

MAGDALENA. How very strange!

    Pause.

PONCIA. Angustias. What did he say to you the first time he came to your window?

ANGUSTIAS. Nothing much. What do you think he'd say? Ordinary things.

MARTIRIO. It really is strange that two people who don't know each other should suddenly meet at a window and the very next thing – they're engaged.

ANGUSTIAS. It didn't surprise me.

AMELIA. I don't know how I would have felt.

ANGUSTIAS. No, because when a man comes to the window, he knows already from people who are always in and out of the house that you'll say 'yes'.

MARTIRIO. Of course. But he had to ask you.

ANGUSTIAS. ¡Claro!

AMELIA (*curiosa*). ¿Y cómo te lo dijo?

ANGUSTIAS. Pues, nada: 'Ya sabes que ando detrás de ti, necesito una mujer buena, modosa, y ésa eres tú, si me das la conformidad.'

AMELIA. ¡A mí me da vergüenza de estas cosas!

ANGUSTIAS. ¡Y a mí, pero hay que pasarlas!

PONCIA. ¿Y habló más?

ANGUSTIAS. Sí, siempre habló él.

MARTIRIO. ¿Y tú?

ANGUSTIAS. Yo no hubiera podido. Casi se me salía el corazón por la boca. Era la primera vez que estaba sola de noche con un hombre.

MAGDALENA. Y un hombre tan guapo.

ANGUSTIAS. ¡No tiene mal tipo!

PONCIA. Esas cosas pasan entre personas ya un poco instruidas que hablan y dicen y mueven la mano ... La primera vez que mi marido Evaristo el Colorín vino a mi ventana ... ¡Ja, ja, ja!

AMELIA. ¿Qué pasó?

PONCIA. Era muy oscuro. Lo vi acercarse y, al llegar, me dijo: 'Buenas noches.' 'Buenas noches', le dije yo, y nos quedamos callados más de media hora. Me corría el sudor por todo el cuerpo. Entonces Evaristo se acercó, se acercó que se quería meter por los hierros, y dijo con voz muy baja: '¡Ven, que te tiente!'

Ríen todas. AMELIA *se levanta corriendo y espía por una puerta.*

AMELIA. ¡Ay! Creí que llegaba nuestra madre.

MAGDALENA. ¡Buenas nos hubiera puesto!

Siguen riendo.

AMELIA. Chiss ... ¡Que nos va a oír!

ANGUSTIAS. Naturally!

AMELIA (*with curiosity*). So how did he ask you?

ANGUSTIAS. Oh, I don't know. He just said: 'You know that I want you, that I need a good, well-behaved woman, and you are the one, if you agree.'

AMELIA. I get so embarrassed by that sort of thing!

ANGUSTIAS. Me too, but you have to put up with it!

PONCIA. Did he say any more?

ANGUSTIAS. Yes, he did all the talking.

MARTIRIO. And you?

ANGUSTIAS. I couldn't have said a thing. My heart was almost coming out of my mouth. It was the first time I'd been alone with a man at night.

MAGDALENA. And such a handsome man.

ANGUSTIAS. He *is* quite good-looking.

PONCIA. That's what happens when you're with someone with a bit of knowledge, who can talk a lot and wave his hands about ... The first time my husband Evaristo el Colorín came to my window ... Ha, ha, ha.

AMELIA. What happened?

PONCIA. It was very dark. I saw him coming and then he said to me: 'Good evening.' 'Good evening,' I said to him, and we were silent for more than half an hour. The sweat was running down my entire body. Then Evaristo came closer and closer, as if he wanted to squeeze through the bars, and he said very quietly: 'Come here, let me feel you!'

> *They all laugh.* AMELIA *gets up, runs to the door and peeps out.*

AMELIA. Oh, I thought Mother was coming.

MAGDALENA. She'd have given us what for!

> *They continue laughing.*

AMELIA. Sh-h-h-h! She'll hear us!

PONCIA. Luego se portó bien. En vez de darle por otra cosa, le dio por criar colorines hasta que murió. A vosotras, que sois solteras, os conviene saber de todos modos que el hombre a los quince días de boda deja la cama por la mesa, y luego la mesa por la tabernilla. Y la que no se conforma se pudre llorando en un rincón.

AMELIA. Tú te conformaste.

PONCIA. ¡Yo pude con él!

MARTIRIO. ¿Es verdad que le pegaste algunas veces?

PONCIA. Sí, y por poco lo dejo tuerto.

MAGDALENA. ¡Así debían ser todas las mujeres!

PONCIA. Yo tengo la escuela de tu madre. Un día me dijo no sé qué cosa y le maté todos los colorines con la mano del almirez.

Ríen.

MAGDALENA. Adela, niña, no te pierdas esto.

AMELIA. Adela.

Pausa.

MAGDALENA. ¡Voy a ver! (*Entra.*)

PONCIA. ¡Esa niña está mala!

MARTIRIO. Claro, ¡no duerme apenas!

PONCIA. Pues, ¿qué hace?

MARTIRIO. ¡Yo qué sé lo que hace!

PONCIA. Mejor lo sabrás tú que yo, que duermes pared por medio.

ANGUSTIAS. La envidia la come.

AMELIA. No exageres.

ANGUSTIAS. Se lo noto en los ojos. Se le está poniendo mirar de loca.

MARTIRIO. No habléis de locos. Aquí es el único sitio donde no se puede pronunciar esta palabra.

PONCIA. Afterwards he behaved himself. Instead of getting any fancy ideas, he took to breeding linnets until he died. You women, being single, ought to know, anyway, that two weeks after the wedding a man leaves the bed for the table, and then the table for the tavern. And the woman who doesn't accept it wastes away crying in a corner.

AMELIA. You accepted it.

PONCIA. I could handle him!

MARTIRIO. Is it true you beat him sometimes?

PONCIA. Yes, and I almost put his eye out.

MAGDALENA. All women should be like that!

PONCIA. I'm of the same school as your mother. One day he said something to me – I can't remember what – and I killed all his linnets with the rolling-pin.

They laugh.

MAGDALENA. Adela, child, you don't know what you're missing.

AMELIA. Adela!

Pause.

MAGDALENA. I'll go and see. (*She goes out.*)

PONCIA. That child is sick!

MARTIRIO. Of course she is! She hardly sleeps!

PONCIA. So what does she do?

MARTIRIO. How do I know what she does?

PONCIA. You must know better than me. You sleep with just a wall between you.

ANGUSTIAS. She's eaten up with envy.

AMELIA. Don't exaggerate.

ANGUSTIAS. I can see it in her eyes. She's starting to get the look of a mad woman.

MARTIRIO. Don't talk about mad people. This is the one place you shouldn't say that word.

Sale MAGDALENA *con* ADELA.

MAGDALENA. Pues, ¿no estabas dormida?

ADELA. Tengo mal cuerpo.

MARTIRIO (*con intención*). ¿Es que no has dormido bien esta noche?

ADELA. Sí.

MARTIRIO. ¿Entonces?

ADELA (*fuerte*). ¡Déjame ya! ¡Durmiendo o velando, no tienes por qué meterte en lo mío! ¡Yo hago con mi cuerpo lo que me parece!

MARTIRIO. ¡Sólo es interés por ti!

ADELA. Interés o inquisición. ¿No estabais cosiendo? Pues seguir. ¡Quisiera ser invisible, pasar por las habitaciones sin que me preguntarais dónde voy!

CRIADA (*entra*). Bernarda os llama. Está el hombre de los encajes.

Salen. Al salir, MARTIRIO *mira fijamente a* ADELA.

ADELA. ¡No me mires más! Si quieres te daré mis ojos, que son frescos, y mis espaldas, para que te compongas la joroba que tienes, pero vuelve la cabeza cuando yo pase.

Se va MARTIRIO.

PONCIA. ¡Adela, que es tu hermana, y además la que más te quiere!

ADELA. Me sigue a todos lados. A veces se asoma a mi cuarto para ver si duermo. No me deja respirar. Y siempre: '¡Qué lástima de cara! ¡Qué lástima de cuerpo, que no va a ser para nadie!' ¡Y eso no! ¡Mi cuerpo será de quien yo quiera!

PONCIA (*con intención y en voz baja*). De Pepe el Romano, ¿no es eso?

ADELA (*sobrecogida*). ¿Qué dices?

MAGDALENA *enters with* ADELA.

MAGDALENA. You weren't asleep, then?

ADELA. I don't feel well.

MARTIRIO (*pointedly*). Didn't you sleep last night?

ADELA. Yes.

MARTIRIO. Well, then?

ADELA (*strongly*). Leave me alone! Asleep or awake, it's my business, nothing to do with you! I'll do what I like with my body.

MARTIRIO. It's only concern for you!

ADELA. Concern or curiosity. Weren't you sewing? Well, why don't you get on with it? I'd like to be invisible! To walk through these rooms, without you asking me where I'm going!

SERVANT (*entering*). Bernarda wants you. The man with the lace is here.

> *They go out. As they do so,* MARTIRIO *stares at* ADELA.

ADELA. Stop staring at me! If you like, I'll give you my bright eyes and my back to improve that hump of yours, but turn your head when I pass.

> MARTIRIO *leaves.*

PONCIA. Adela, she's your sister and, what's more, the one who loves you most.

ADELA. She follows me everywhere. Sometimes she looks into my room to see if I'm asleep. She doesn't let me breathe. And always: 'What a shame about that face! What a shame about that body, that will never belong to anyone!' It isn't true. My body will be for whoever I please!

PONCIA (*pointedly and quietly*). You mean for Pepe el Romano?

ADELA (*taken aback*). What do you mean?

PONCIA. ¡Lo que digo, Adela!

ADELA. ¡Calla!

PONCIA (*alto*). ¿Crees que no me he fijado?

ADELA. ¡Baja la voz!

PONCIA. ¡Mata esos pensamientos!

ADELA. ¿Qué sabes tú?

PONCIA. Las viejas vemos a través de las paredes. ¿Dónde vas de noche cuando te levantas?

ADELA. ¡Ciega debías estar!

PONCIA. Con la cabeza y las manos llenas de ojos cuando se trata de lo que se trata. Por mucho que pienso no sé lo que te propones. ¿Por qué te pusiste casi desnuda con la luz encendida y la ventana abierta al pasar Pepe el segundo día que vino a hablar con tu hermana?

ADELA. ¡Eso no es verdad!

PONCIA. ¡No seas como los niños chicos! Deja en paz a tu hermana y si Pepe el Romano te gusta te aguantas. (ADELA *llora*.) Además, ¿quién dice que no te puedas casar con él? Tu hermana Angustias es una enferma. Esa no resiste el primer parto. Es estrecha de cintura, vieja, y con mi conocimiento te digo que se morirá. Entonces Pepe hará lo que hacen todos los viudos de esta tierra: se casará con la más joven, la más hermosa, y ésa eres tú. Alimenta esa esperanza, olvídalo. Lo que quieras, pero no vayas contra la ley de Dios.

ADELA. ¡Calla!

PONCIA. ¡No callo!

ADELA. Métete en tus cosas, ¡oledora! ¡pérfida!

PONCIA. ¡Sombra tuya he de ser!

ADELA. En vez de limpiar la casa y acostarte para rezar a tus muertos, buscas como una vieja marrana asuntos de hombres y mujeres para babosear en ellos.

PONCIA. What I say, Adela!

ADELA. Be quiet!

PONCIA (*loudly*). Do you think I haven't noticed?

ADELA. Lower your voice!

PONCIA. Put such thoughts out of your head.

ADELA. What do you know?

PONCIA. We old women can see through walls. Where do you go at night when you get up?

ADELA. I wish you were blind!

PONCIA. My head and my hands are nothing but eyes in matters like these. For the life of me, I don't know what you're up to. Why were you standing almost naked, with the lamp lit and the window open, when Pepe passed the second time he came to speak with your sister?

ADELA. That isn't true!

PONCIA. Don't be childish! Leave your sister in peace, and if you like Pepe el Romano, resign yourself. (ADELA *weeps*.) Besides, who says you can't marry him? Your sister Angustias is delicate. She won't survive the first birth. She's narrow-waisted, getting on in years, and from my experience I can tell you she'll die. Then Pepe will do what all the widowers do around here: he'll marry the youngest, the prettiest, and that's you. Cling to that hope, forget him – whatever you like, but don't go against the will of God.

ADELA. Be quiet!

PONCIA. I won't be quiet!

ADELA. Mind your own business, you nosy, scheming old hag!

PONCIA. I shall be your shadow!

ADELA. Instead of cleaning the house and going to bed to pray for your dead, you stick your nose like an old sow into men and women's affairs, so you can drool over them.

PONCIA. ¡Velo!, para que las gentes no escupan al pasar por esta puerta.

ADELA. ¡Qué cariño tan grande te ha entrado de pronto por mi hermana!

PONCIA. No os tengo ley a ninguna, pero quiero vivir en casa decente. ¡No quiero mancharme de vieja!

ADELA. Es inútil tu consejo. Ya es tarde. No por encima de ti, que eres una criada, por encima de mi madre saltaría para apagarme este fuego que tengo levantado por piernas y boca. ¿Qué puedes decir de mí? ¿Que me encierro en mi cuarto y no abro la puerta? ¿Que no duermo? ¡Soy más lista que tú! Mira a ver si puedes agarrar la liebre con tus manos.

PONCIA. No me desafíes. ¡Adela, no me desafíes! Porque yo puedo dar voces, encender luces y hacer que toquen las campanas.

ADELA. Trae cuatro mil bengalas amarillas y ponlas en las bardas del corral. Nadie podrá evitar que suceda lo que tiene que suceder.

PONCIA. ¡Tanto te gusta ese hombre!

ADELA. ¡Tanto! Mirando sus ojos me parece que bebo su sangre lentamente.

PONCIA. Yo no te puedo oír.

ADELA. ¡Pues me oirás! Te he tenido miedo. ¡Pero ya soy más fuerte que tú!

Entra ANGUSTIAS.

ANGUSTIAS. ¡Siempre discutiendo!

PONCIA. Claro, se empeña en que, con el calor que hace, vaya a traerle no sé qué cosa de la tienda.

ANGUSTIAS. ¿Me compraste el bote de esencia?

PONCIA. El más caro. Y los polvos. En la mesa de tu cuarto los he puesto.

Sale ANGUSTIAS.

PONCIA. I keep watch! so that people can't spit as they pass this door.

ADELA. Why all this sudden affection for my sister?

PONCIA. I feel no loyalty for any of you, but I want to live in a respectable house. I don't want to be disgraced in my old age!

ADELA. Your advice is pointless. It's too late already. I'd leap right over you. You're only a servant. And I'd leap over my mother too . . . anything to put out this fire that rises up through my legs and my mouth. What can you say about me? That I lock myself in my room? That I don't open the door? That I don't sleep? I'm smarter than you! See if you can catch the hare with your hands.

PONCIA. Don't defy me! Adela, don't defy me! I can call out, light lamps and make the bells ring.

ADELA. Bring four thousand yellow flares and put them on the walls of the stable-yard. What will be will be. No one can stop it.

PONCIA. You want the man as much as that!

ADELA. That much! Looking into his eyes is just like slowly drinking his blood!

PONCIA. I can't listen to you!

ADELA. Well, you shall listen to me! I was afraid of you. But now I'm stronger than you are!

ANGUSTIAS *enters.*

ANGUSTIAS. Always arguing!

PONCIA. Yes. She wants me to get her something from the shop in all this heat.

ANGUSTIAS. Did you buy the bottle of perfume for me?

PONCIA. The most expensive one. And the face-powder. I put them on the table in your room.

ANGUSTIAS *leaves.*

ADELA. ¡Y chitón!

PONCIA. ¡Lo veremos!

Entran MARTIRIO, AMELIA *y* MAGDALENA.

MAGDALENA (*a* ADELA). ¿Has visto los encajes?

AMELIA. Los de Angustias para sus sábanas de novia son preciosos.

ADELA (*a* MARTIRIO, *que trae unos encajes*). ¿Y éstos?

MARTIRIO. Son para mí. Para una camisa.

ADELA (*con sarcasmo*). ¡Se necesita buen humor!

MARTIRIO (*con intención*). Para verlos yo. No necesito lucirme ante nadie.

PONCIA. Nadie la ve a una en camisa.

MARTIRIO (*con intención y mirando a* ADELA). ¡A veces! Pero me encanta la ropa interior. Si fuera rica la tendría de holanda. Es uno de los pocos gustos que me quedan.

PONCIA. Estos encajes son preciosos para las gorras de niño, para manteruelos de cristianar. Yo nunca pude usarlos en los míos. A ver si ahora Angustias los usa en los suyos. Como le dé por tener crías vais a estar cosiendo mañana y tarde.

MAGDALENA. Yo no pienso dar una puntada.

AMELIA. Y mucho menos cuidar niños ajenos. Mira tú cómo están las vecinas del callejón, sacrificadas por cuatro monigotes.

PONCIA. Esas están mejor que vosotras. ¡Siquiera allí se ríe y se oyen porrazos!

MARTIRIO. Pues vete a servir con ellas.

PONCIA. No. ¡Ya me ha tocado en suerte este convento!

Se oyen unos campanillos lejanos, como a través de varios muros.

MAGDALENA. Son los hombres que vuelven al trabajo.

PONCIA. Hace un minuto dieron las tres.

ADELA. Not a word!

PONCIA. We'll see about that!

MARTIRIO, AMELIA *and* MAGDALENA *enter.*

MAGDALENA (*to* ADELA). Have you seen the lace?

AMELIA. The lace for Angustias' wedding sheets is just beautiful.

ADELA (*to* MARTIRIO, *who is holding some lace*). And this?

MARTIRIO. It's for me. For a petticoat.

ADELA (*sarcastically*). One has to have a sense of humour!

MARTIRIO (*pointedly*). For me to look at. I don't need to flaunt myself to anyone.

PONCIA. No one sees you in your petticoat.

MARTIRIO (*pointedly, looking at* ADELA). They do . . . sometimes! I adore underwear. If I were rich, I'd have it all made of Dutch linen. It's one of the few pleasures I've still got left.

PONCIA. This lace is perfect for a baby's bonnet, or for a christening gown. I could never dress mine in it. Let's see if Angustias can use it for hers. If she starts having children, you'll be sewing day and night.

MAGDALENA. I don't intend to sew a stitch!

AMELIA. Even less look after someone else's children. Look at the women down the street, martyrs to their little brats.

PONCIA. They are better off than you are. At least they have a laugh down there and a bit of a scuffle.

MARTIRIO. So go and work for them.

PONCIA. No. It's been my lot to serve in this convent.

Distant bells are heard, as through several walls.

MAGDALENA. It's the men going back to work.

PONCIA. It struck three just a minute ago.

MARTIRIO. ¡Con este sol!

ADELA (*sentándose*). ¡Ay, quién pudiera salir también a los campos!

MAGDALENA (*sentándose*). ¡Cada clase tiene que hacer lo suyo!

MARTIRIO (*sentándose*). ¡Así es!

AMELIA (*sentándose*). ¡Ay!

PONCIA. No hay alegría como la de los campos en esta época. Ayer de mañana llegaron los segadores. Cuarenta o cincuenta buenos mozos.

MAGDALENA. ¿De dónde son este año?

PONCIA. De muy lejos. Vinieron de los montes. ¡Alegres! ¡Como árboles quemados! ¡Dando voces y arrojando piedras! Anoche llegó al pueblo una mujer vestida de lentejuelas y que bailaba con un acordeón, y quince de ellos la contrataron para llevársela al olivar. Yo los vi de lejos. El que la contrataba era un muchacho de ojos verdes, apretado como una gavilla de trigo.

AMELIA. ¿Es eso cierto?

ADELA. ¡Pero es posible!

PONCIA. Hace años vino otra de éstas y yo misma di dinero a mi hijo mayor para que fuera. Los hombres necesitan estas cosas.

ADELA. Se les perdona todo.

AMELIA. Nacer mujer es el mayor castigo.

MAGDALENA. Y ni nuestros ojos siquiera nos pertenecen.

Se oye un canto lejano que se va acercando.

PONCIA. Son ellos. Traen unos cantos preciosos.

AMELIA. Ahora salen a segar.

CORO.
Ya salen los segadores
en busca de las espigas;
se llevan los corazones
de las muchachas que miran.

MARTIRIO. In this heat!

ADELA (*sitting down*). Oh, if I could only go out to the fields too!

MAGDALENA (*sitting down*). Each class does what it must.

MARTIRIO (*sitting down*). That's how things are!

AMELIA (*sitting down*). I'm afraid so.

PONCIA. There's nothing like being in the fields at this time of year. The harvesters came yesterday morning. Forty or fifty fine young men.

MAGDALENA. Where are they from this year?

PONCIA. From a long way away. They came from the mountains. Full of joy! Their skin the colour of burnt trees. Shouting and throwing stones! Last night a woman arrived in the village dressed in sequins. She was dancing to the accordion, and fifteen of them hired her and took her with them to the olive-grove. I saw them from a long way off. The one who was arranging it was a boy with green eyes, firm as a sheaf of wheat.

AMELIA. Is that true?

ADELA. Of course it is!

PONCIA. Years ago another of these women came and I myself gave money to my eldest son so he could go with her. Men need these things.

ADELA. They are forgiven everything!

AMELIA. To be born a woman is the greatest punishment.

MAGDALENA. Even our eyes aren't our own.

Distant singing is heard, coming closer.

PONCIA. It's them. They have some beautiful songs.

AMELIA. They are going out to reap now.

CHORUS.
  The reapers go out to the fields now,
  They go for the harvesting;
  And as they go they take with them
  The hearts of the girls who are watching.

Se oyen panderos y carrañacas. Pausa. Todas oyen en
un silencio traspasado por el sol.

AMELIA. ¡Y no les importa el calor!

MARTIRIO. Siegan entre llamaradas.

ADELA. Me gustaría segar para ir y venir. Así se olvida lo
que nos muerde.

MARTIRIO. ¿Qué tienes tú que olvidar?

ADELA. Cada una sabe sus cosas.

MARTIRIO (*profunda*). ¡Cada una!

PONCIA. ¡Callar! ¡Callar!

CORO (*muy lejano*).
  Abrir puertas y ventanas
  las que vivís en el pueblo;
  el segador pide rosas
  para adornar su sombrero.

PONCIA. ¡Qué canto!

MARTIRIO (*con nostalgia*).
  Abrir puertas y ventanas
  las que vivís en el pueblo.

ADELA (*con pasión*).
  El segador pide rosas
  para adornar su sombrero.

Se va alejando el cantar.

PONCIA. Ahora dan la vuelta a la esquina.

ADELA. Vamos a verlos por la ventana de mi cuarto.

PONCIA. Tened cuidado con no entreabrirla mucho,
porque son capaces de dar un empujón para ver quién
mira.

Se van las tres. MARTIRIO *queda sentada en la silla*
baja con la cabeza entre las manos.

AMELIA (*acercándose*). ¿Qué te pasa?

MARTIRIO. Me sienta mal el calor.

*Tambourines and carrañacas are heard. Pause. All
the women listen in a silence peirced by the sunlight.*

AMELIA. The heat doesn't bother them.

MARTIRIO. They reap in tongues of fire.

ADELA. I'd like to be a reaper so I could come and go as I
please. Then I'd forget what's gnawing away at us.

MARTIRIO. What do *you* have to forget?

ADELA. Each one of us knows her own heart.

MARTIRIO (*with feeling*). Each one of us!

PONCIA. Be quiet! Be quiet!

CHORUS (*very distant*).

Open your doors and windows,
You girls who live in the town.
The reaper wants your roses
To decorate his crown.

PONCIA. Such a lovely song!

MARTIRIO (*with nostalgia*).

Open your doors and windows,
You girls who live in the town . . .

ADELA (*passionately*).

. . . The reaper wants your roses
To decorate his crown.

The singing grows distant.

PONCIA. They are turning the corner.

ADELA. Let's go and see them from the window of my
room.

PONCIA. Take care not to open it too much, or they'll give
it a push to see who's looking.

The three of them leave. MARTIRIO *remains seated
on the low chair, with her head in her hands.*

AMELIA (*approaching*). What's wrong?

MARTIRIO. This heat is getting me down.

AMELIA. ¿No es más que eso?

MARTIRIO. Estoy deseando que llegue noviembre, los días de lluvia, la escarcha; todo lo que no sea este verano interminable.

AMELIA. Ya pasará y volverá otra vez.

MARTIRIO. ¡Claro! (*Pausa.*) ¿A qué hora te dormiste anoche?

AMELIA. No sé. Yo duermo como un tronco. ¿Por qué?

MARTIRIO. Por nada, pero me pareció oír gente en el corral.

AMELIA. ¿Sí?

MARTIRIO. Muy tarde.

AMELIA. ¿Y no tuviste miedo?

MARTIRIO. No. Ya lo he oído otras noches.

AMELIA. Debíamos tener cuidado. ¿No serían los gañanes?

MARTIRIO. Los gañanes llegan a las seis.

AMELIA. Quizá una mulilla sin desbravar.

MARTIRIO (*entre dientes y llena de segunda intención*). Eso, ¡eso!, una mulilla sin desbravar.

AMELIA. ¡Hay que prevenir!

MARTIRIO. ¡No, no! No digas nada. Puede ser un volunto mío.

AMELIA. Quizá.

Pausa. AMELIA *inicia el mutis.*

MARTIRIO. Amelia.

AMELIA (*en la puerta*). ¿Qué?

Pausa.

MARTIRIO. Nada.

Pausa.

AMELIA. ¿Por qué me llamaste?

Pausa.

AMELIA. Are you sure it isn't something else?

MARTIRIO. I can't wait for November to come, the wet days, the frost; anything but this endless summer!

AMELIA. When it's gone it will soon come round again.

MARTIRIO. Yes! (*Pause.*) What time did you go to sleep last night?

AMELIA. I don't know. I sleep like a log. Why?

MARTIRIO. Oh, nothing, but I thought I heard people in the stable-yard.

AMELIA. Really?

MARTIRIO. Very late.

AMELIA. Weren't you scared?

MARTIRIO. No, I've heard it other nights.

AMELIA. We'll have to be careful. Could it have been the farmhands?

MARTIRIO. They come at six.

AMELIA. Pehaps a young mule still to be broken in.

MARTIRIO (*to herself, with a double meaning*). Yes, that's it! A young mule still to be broken in.

AMELIA. We'd better warn the others.

MARTIRIO. No, no! Don't say anything. I might have imagined it.

AMELIA. Maybe.

Pause. AMELIA *starts to leave.*

MARTIRIO. Amelia.

AMELIA (*at the door*). What?

Pause.

MARTIRIO. Nothing.

Pause.

AMELIA. Why did you call me?

Pause.

MARTIRIO. Se me escapó. Fue sin darme cuenta.

Pausa.

AMELIA. Acuéstate un poco.

ANGUSTIAS (*entrando furiosa en escena, de modo que haya un gran contraste con los silencios anteriores*). ¿Dónde está el retrato de Pepe que tenía yo debajo de mi almohada? ¿Quién de vosotras lo tiene?

MARTIRIO. Ninguna.

AMELIA. Ni que Pepe fuera un San Bartolomé de plata.

Entran PONCIA, MAGDALENA *y* ADELA.

ANGUSTIAS. ¿Dónde está el retrato?

ADELA. ¿Qué retrato?

ANGUSTIAS. Una de vosotras me lo ha escondido.

MAGDALENA. ¿Tienes la desvergüenza de decir esto?

ANGUSTIAS. Estaba en mi cuarto y no está.

MARTIRIO. ¿Y no se habrá escapado a medianoche al corral? A Pepe le gusta andar con la luna.

ANGUSTIAS. ¡No me gastes bromas! Cuando venga se lo contaré.

PONCIA. ¡Eso, no! ¡Porque aparecerá! (*Mirando a* ADELA.)

ANGUSTIAS. ¡Me gustaría saber cuál de vosotras lo tiene!

ADELA (*mirando a* MARTIRIO). ¡Alguna! ¡Todas, menos yo!

MARTIRIO (*con intención*). ¡Desde luego!

BERNARDA (*entrando con su bastón*). ¡Qué escándalo es éste en mi casa y con el silencio del peso del calor! Estarán las vecinas con el oído pegado a los tabiques.

ANGUSTIAS. Me han quitado el retrato de mi novio.

BERNARDA (*fiera*). ¿Quién? ¿Quién?

ANGUSTIAS. ¡Estas!

MARTIRIO. It slipped out. I wasn't thinking.

Pause.

AMELIA. Lie down for a while.

ANGUSTIAS (*entering furiously, so that there is a great contrast with the earlier silences*). Where's the picture of Pepe that was under my pillow? Which of you has it?

MARTIRIO. None of us.

AMELIA. It's not as if Pepe were a silver Saint Bartholomew!

PONCIA, MAGDALENA *and* ADELA *enter.*

ANGUSTIAS. Where is the picture?

ADELA. What picture?

ANGUSTIAS. One of you has hidden it.

MAGDALENA. You have the cheek to say that?

ANGUSTIAS. It was in my room and now it's not.

MARTIRIO. It might have slipped out into the stable-yard at midnight. Pepe likes to walk in the moonlight.

ANGUSTIAS. Don't play tricks on me! When he comes, I'll tell him.

PONCIA. Don't do that! It will turn up! (*Looking at* ADELA.)

ANGUSTIAS. I want to know which one of you has it!

ADELA (*looking at* MARTIRIO). Someone has! Any one of us, but not me!

MARTIRIO (*pointedly*). Not her, naturally!

BERNARDA (*entering with her stick*). What noise is this in my house? There's not a sound outside in this stifling heat. The neighbours will have their ears glued to the walls.

ANGUSTIAS. They've stolen my fiancé's picture.

BERNARDA (*fiercely*). Who? Who?

ANGUSTIAS. Them!

BERNARDA. ¿Cuál de vosotras? (*Silencio.*) ¡Contestarme! (*Silencio. A* PONCIA.) Registra los cuartos, mira por las camas. Esto tiene no ataros más cortas. ¡Pero me vais a soñar! (*A* ANGUSTIAS.) ¿Estás segura?

ANGUSTIAS. Sí.

BERNARDA. ¿Lo has buscado bien?

ANGUSTIAS. Sí, madre.

> *Todas están de pie en medio de un embarazoso silencio.*

BERNARDA. Me hacéis al final de mi vida beber el veneno más amargo que una madre puede resistir. (*A* PONCIA.) ¿No lo encuentras?

> *Sale* PONCIA.

PONCIA. Aquí está.

BERNARDA. ¿Dónde lo has encontrado?

PONCIA. Estaba . . .

BERNARDA. Dilo sin temor.

PONCIA (*extrañada*). Entre las sábanas de la cama de Martirio.

BERNARDA (*a* MARTIRIO). ¿Es verdad?

MARTIRIO. ¡Es verdad!

BERNARDA (*avanzando y golpeándola con el bastón*). ¡Mala puñalada te den, mosca muerta! ¡Sembradura de vidrios!

MARTIRIO (*fiera*). ¡No me pegue usted, madre!

BERNARDA. ¡Todo lo que quiera!

MARTIRIO. ¡Si yo la dejo! ¿Lo oye? ¡Retírese usted!

PONCIA. No faltes a tu madre.

ANGUSTIAS (*cogiendo a* BERNARDA). Déjela. ¡Por favor!

BERNARDA. Ni lágrimas te quedan en esos ojos.

MARTIRIO. No voy a llorar para darle gusto.

BERNARDA. ¿Por qué has cogido el retrato?

BERNARDA. Which of you? (*Silence.*) Answer me! (*Silence. To* PONCIA.) Search the rooms, look in the beds! This comes from not keeping you on a shorter leash. But I shall haunt you all in your dreams! (*To* ANGUSTIAS.) Are you sure?

ANGUSTIAS. Yes.

BERNARDA. Have you had a really good look for it?

ANGUSTIAS. Yes, Mother.

They are all standing. An awkward silence.

BERNARDA. So, in my old age, you are making me, your mother, drink the bitterest poison. (*To* PONCIA.) Can't you find it?

PONCIA (*entering*). Here it is!

BERNARDA. Where did you find it?

PONCIA. It was . . .

BERNARDA. Tell me, don't be afraid!

PONCIA (*disbelieving*). Between the sheets of Martirio's bed.

BERNARDA (*to* MARTIRIO). Is that true?

MARTIRIO. Yes, it is!

BERNARDA (*advancing, striking her with the stick*). Damn you, you sly creature! Nothing but a troublemaker!

MARTIRIO (*fiercely*). Don't hit me, Mother!

BERNARDA. I'll hit you as much as I like!

MARTIRIO. I shan't let you! Do you hear? Get away from me!

PONCIA. Have some respect for your mother.

ANGUSTIAS (*holding* BERNARDA). Leave her alone! Please!

BERNARDA. Not a tear in those eyes!

MARTIRIO. I shan't cry to satisfy you.

BERNARDA. Why did you take the picture?

MARTIRIO. ¿Es que yo no puedo gastar una broma a mi hermana? ¡Para qué otra cosa lo iba a querer!

ADELA (*saltando llena de celos*). No ha sido broma, que tú no has gustado jamás de juegos. Ha sido otra cosa que te reventaba en el pecho por querer salir. Dilo ya claramente.

MARTIRIO. ¡Calla y no me hagas hablar, que si hablo se van a juntar las paredes unas con otras de vergüenza!

ADELA. ¡La mala lengua no tiene fin para inventar!

BERNARDA. ¡Adela!

MAGDALENA. Estáis locas.

AMELIA. Y nos apedreáis con malos pensamientos.

MARTIRIO. Otras hacen cosas más malas.

ADELA. Hasta que se pongan en cueros de una vez y se las lleve el río.

BERNARDA. ¡Perversa!

ANGUSTIAS. Yo no tengo la culpa de que Pepe el Romano se haya fijado en mí.

ADELA. ¡Por tus dineros!

ANGUSTIAS. ¡Madre!

BERNARDA. ¡Silencio!

MARTIRIO. Por tus marjales y tus arboledas.

MAGDALENA. ¡Eso es lo justo!

BERNARDA. ¡Silencio digo! Yo veía la tormenta venir, pero no creía que estallara tan pronto. ¡Ay, qué pedrisco de odio habéis echado sobre mi corazón! Pero todavía no soy anciana y tengo cinco cadenas para vosotras y esta casa levantada por mi padre para que ni las hierbas se enteren de mi desolación. ¡Fuera de aquí!

> *Salen.* BERNARDA *se sienta desolada.* PONCIA *está de pie arrimada a los muros.* BERNARDA *reacciona, da un golpe en el suelo y dice*:

¡Tendré que sentarles la mano! Bernarda, ¡acuérdate que ésta es tu obligación!

MARTIRIO. Can't I even play a joke on my sister? Why else would I want it?

ADELA (*exploding with jealousy*). It wasn't a joke! You've never liked jokes! It was something else that was boiling inside, wanting to burst out. Admit it!

MARTIRIO. Be quiet! Don't make me speak! If I speak, the walls will close in from shame!

ADELA. There's no end to what an evil tongue will invent!

BERNARDA. Adela!

MAGDALENA. You are both mad.

AMELIA. And you shower us with your evil thoughts.

MARTIRIO. There are others who do far worse things.

ADELA. Until they are suddenly naked and let the current take them.

BERNARDA. You shameless creature!

ANGUSTIAS. It's not my fault that Pepe el Romano's chosen me.

ADELA. For your money!

ANGUSTIAS. Mother!

BERNARDA. Silence!

MARTIRIO. For your land and your orchards!

MAGDALENA. It's true!

BERNARDA. Silence, I say! I could see the storm coming, but I never thought it would break so soon. Oh, what a hailstorm of hate you have poured on my heart! But I'm not an old women yet. I've got five chains – for each of you, and these walls my father built, so even the weeds can never learn of my desolation. Get out of here!

> *They leave.* BERNARDA *sits in despair.* PONCIA *is standing close to the wall.* BERNARDA *composes herself, bangs the floor and says*:

I shall have to take a firm grip! Bernarda, remember it's your duty.

PONCIA. ¿Puedo hablar?

BERNARDA. Habla. Siento que hayas oído. Nunca está bien una extraña en el centro de la familia.

PONCIA. Lo visto, visto está.

BERNARDA. Angustias tiene que casarse en seguida.

PONCIA. Claro, hay que retirarla de aquí.

BERNARDA. No a ella. ¡A él!

PONCIA. Claro, ¡a él hay que alejarlo de aquí! Piensas bien.

BERNARDA. No pienso. Hay cosas que no se pueden ni se deben pensar. Yo ordeno.

PONCIA. ¿Y tú crees que él querrá marcharse?

BERNARDA (levantándose). ¿Qué imagina tu cabeza?

PONCIA. El, claro, ¡se casará con Angustias!

BERNARDA. Habla. Te conozco demasidado para saber que ya me tienes preparada la cuchilla.

PONCIA. Nunca pensé que se llamara asesinato al aviso.

BERNARDA. ¿Me tienes que prevenir algo?

PONCIA. Yo no acuso, Bernarda. Yo sólo te digo: abre los ojos y verás.

BERNARDA. ¿Y verás qué?

PONCIA. Siempre has sido lista. Has visto lo malo de las gentes a cien leguas. Muchas veces creí que adivinabas los pensamientos. Pero los hijos son los hijos. Ahora estás ciega.

BERNARDA. ¿Te refieres a Martirio?

PONCIA. Bueno, a Martirio . . . (Con curiosidad.) ¿Por qué habrá escondido el retrato?

BERNARDA (queriendo ocultar a su hija). Después de todo ella dice que ha sido una broma. ¿Qué otra cosa puede ser?

PONCIA (con sorna). ¿Tú lo crees así?

BERNARDA (enérgica). No lo creo. ¡Es así!

PONCIA. May I speak?

BERNARDA. Speak. I'm sorry that you heard. It's never good to have an outsider inside the family.

PONCIA. What I've seen, I've seen.

BERNARDA. Angustias has to get married at once.

PONCIA. Yes, you have to get her away from here.

BERNARDA. Not her! Him!

PONCIA. Of course, you have to get *him* away from here! That's very good thinking.

BERNARDA. I don't 'think'. There are things you can't and shouldn't think. I command.

PONCIA. And do you think he'll want to go?

BERNARDA (*getting up*). What's going on in that head of yours?

PONCIA. He, of course, will marry Angustias!

BERNARDA. Speak. I know you well enough to see you have the knife ready.

PONCIA. I never thought a warning could be called murder.

BERNARDA. Is there something you have to warn me about?

PONCIA. I'm not accusing you, Bernarda. I'm only telling you: open your eyes and you'll see.

BERNARDA. See what?

PONCIA. You've always been clever. You've seen the bad in people a hundred miles away. I often felt you could read their thoughts. But it's different with your children. Now you are blind.

BERNARDA. You mean Martirio?

PONCIA. Yes, well, Martirio ... (*Inquisitively.*) Why would she hide the picture?

BERNARDA (*wanting to protect her daughter*). She says it was a joke. What else could it be?

PONCIA (*sarcastically*). You really believe that?

BERNARDA (*forcefully*). I don't believe it. It's true!

PONCIA. Basta. Se trata de lo tuyo. Pero si fuera la vecina de enfrente, ¿qué sería?

BERNARDA. Ya empiezas a sacar la punta del cuchillo.

PONCIA (*siempre con crueldad*). No, Bernarda: aquí pasa una cosa muy grande. Yo no te quiero echar la culpa, pero tú no has dejado a tus hijas libres. Martirio es enamoradiza, digas tú lo que quieras. ¿Por qué no la dejaste casar con Enrique Humanes? ¿Por qué el mismo día que iba a venir a la ventana le mandaste recado que no viniera?

BERNARDA (*fuerte*). ¡Y lo haría mil veces. Mi sangre no se junta con la de los Humanes mientras yo viva! Su padre fue gañán.

PONCIA. ¡Y así te va a ti con esos humos!

BERNARDA. Los tengo porque puedo tenerlos. Y tú no los tienes porque sabes muy bien cuál es tu origen.

PONCIA (*con odio*). ¡No me lo recuerdes! Estoy ya vieja. Siempre agradecí tu protección.

BERNARDA (*crecida*). ¡No lo parece!

PONCIA (*con odio envuelto en suavidad*). A Martirio se le olvidará esto.

BERNARDA. Y si no lo olvida peor para ella. No creo que ésta sea la 'cosa muy grande' que aquí pasa. Aquí no pasa nada. ¡Eso quisieras tú! Y si pasara algún día estáte segura que no traspasaría las paredes.

PONCIA. ¡Eso no lo sé yo! En el pueblo hay gentes que leen también de lejos los pensamientos escondidos.

BERNARDA. ¡Cómo gozarías de vernos a mí y a mis hijas camino del lupanar!

PONCIA. ¡Nadie puede conocer su fin!

BERNARDA. ¡Yo sí sé mi fin! ¡Y el de mis hijas! El lupanar se queda para alguna mujer ya difunta . . .

PONCIA. All right. It's your family. But if it was your neighbour opposite, what then?

BERNARDA. Now you are starting to draw the knife.

PONCIA (*with sustained cruelty*). No, Bernarda: there's something serious happening here. I don't want to blame you, but you haven't given your daughters any freedom. Martirio's prone to falling in love, whatever you say. Why didn't you let her marry Enrique Humanes? Why, on the very day he was going to come to her window, did you send him a message not to come?

BERNARDA (*strongly*). I'd do it a thousand times! My blood shan't mix with Humanes blood as long as I live! His father was a farmhand.

PONCIA. And where have all your airs and graces got you?

BERNARDA. I have them because I can afford them. And you do not because you know what your origins were!

PONCIA (*with hatred*). Don't remind me! I'm an old woman now. I've always been grateful for your protection.

BERNARDA (*imperiously*). It doesn't seem like that!

PONCIA (*her hatred wrapped in sweet words*). Martirio will forget this.

BERNARDA. If she doesn't forget it, the worse for her. I don't believe that there's 'something serious' happening here. There is nothing happening here. That's what you'd like! And if one day it were to happen, be sure it wouldn't go beyond these walls.

PONCIA. I don't know about that! In the village there are people who can read hidden thoughts from far away.

BERNARDA. Oh, how you'd love to see me and my daughters on the way to the whorehouse!

PONCIA. No one can know her end!

BERNARDA. I know mine! And my daughters'! The whorehouse is reserved for a certain dead woman . . .

PONCIA (*fiera*). ¡Bernarda, respeta la memoria de mi madre!

BERNARDA. ¡No me persigas tú con tus malos pensamientos!

Pausa.

PONCIA. Mejor será que no me meta en nada.

BERNARDA. Es lo que debías hacer. Obrar y callar a todo es la obligación de los que viven a sueldo.

PONCIA. Pero no se puede. ¿A ti no te parece que Pepe estaría mejor casado con Martirio o ... ¡sí!, o con Adela?

BERNARDA. No me parece.

PONCIA (*con intención*). Adela. ¡Esa es la verdadera novia del Romano!

BERNARDA. Las cosas no son nunca a gusto nuestro.

PONCIA. Pero les cuesta mucho trabajo desviarse de la verdadera inclinación. A mí me parece mal que Pepe esté con Angustias, y a las gentes, y hasta al aire. ¡Quién sabe si se saldrán con la suya!

BERNARDA. ¡Ya estamos otra vez! ... Te deslizas para llenarme de malos sueños. Y no quiero entenderte, porque si llegara al alcance de todo lo que dices te tendría que arañar.

PONCIA. ¡No llegará la sangre al río!

BERNARDA. ¡Afortunadamente mis hijas me respetan y jamás torcieron mi voluntad!

PONCIA. ¡Eso sí! Pero en cuanto las dejes sueltas se te subirán al tejado.

BERNARDA. ¡Ya las bajaré tirándoles cantos!

PONCIA. ¡Desde luego eres la más valiente!

BERNARDA. ¡Siempre gasté sabrosa pimienta!

PONCIA. ¡Pero lo que son las cosas! A su edad, ¡hay que ver el entusiasmo de Angustias con su novio! ¡Y él también parece muy picado! Ayer me contó mi hijo

PONCIA (*fiercely*). Bernarda, respect my mother's memory!

BERNARDA. Then stop hounding me with your evil thoughts!

Pause.

PONCIA. It's best if I keep out of everything.

BERNARDA. It's what you ought to do. Work and keep your mouth shut. It's the duty of those who are paid to work.

PONCIA. But I can't. Don't you think that Pepe would be better married to Martirio or . . . yes, Adela?

BERNARDA. I don't think so.

PONCIA (*pointedly*). Adela. She's el Romano's true fiancé!

BERNARDA. Things are never as we want them.

PONCIA. But it's hard for people to go against their true nature. It seems wrong to me that Pepe should be with Angustias. Other people, even Nature herself would agree. Who knows if they'll get what they want?

BERNARDA. Here we go again! . . . You creep up to fill me with bad dreams. I don't want to know. If I fully accepted what you are saying, I'd have to tear you to pieces.

PONCIA. It won't come to that.

BERNARDA. Fortunately, my daughters respect me. They have never gone against my wishes.

PONCIA. That's true. But as soon as you set them free they'll fly to the rooftops.

BERNARDA. And I'll bring them down with stones!

PONCIA. Well, you were always the bravest!

BERNARDA. I've always fought the good fight!

PONCIA. But things can be so strange! At her age, you should see how keen Angustias is on her fiancé! And he seems very smitten too. Yesterday my eldest son told me

mayor que a las cuatro y media de la madrugada, que pasó por la calle con la yunta, estaban hablando todavía.

BERNARDA. ¡A las cuatro y media!

ANGUSTIAS (*saliendo*). ¡Mentira!

PONCIA. Eso me contaron.

BERNARDA (*a* ANGUSTIAS). ¡Habla!

ANGUSTIAS. Pepe lleva más de una semana marchándose a la una. Que Dios me mate si miento.

MARTIRIO (*saliendo*). Yo también lo sentí marcharse a las cuatro.

BERNARDA. ¿Pero lo viste con tus ojos?

MARTIRIO. No quise asomarme. ¿No habláis ahora por la ventana del callejón?

ANGUSTIAS. Yo hablo por la ventana de mi dormitorio.

Aparece ADELA *en la puerta.*

MARTIRIO. Entonces . . .

BERNARDA. ¿Qué es lo que pasa aquí?

PONCIA. ¡Cuida de enterarte! Pero, desde luego, Pepe estaba a las cuatro de la madrugada en una reja de tu casa.

BERNARDA. ¿Lo sabes seguro?

PONCIA. Seguro no se sabe nada en esta vida.

ADELA. Madre, no oiga usted a quien nos quiere perder a todas.

BERNARDA. ¡Ya sabré enterarme! Si las gentes del pueblo quieren levantar falsos testimonios se encontrarán con mi pedernal. No se hable de este asunto. Hay a veces una ola de fango que levantan los demás para perdernos.

MARTIRIO. A mí no me gusta mentir.

PONCIA. Y algo habrá.

BERNARDA. No habrá nada. Nací para tener los ojos abiertos. Ahora vigilaré sin cerrarlos ya hasta que me muera.

that when he went past with the oxen, they were still talking at half-past four in the morning.

BERNARDA. At half-past four!

ANGUSTIAS (*entering*). It's a lie!

PONCIA. That's what they told me.

BERNARDA (*to* ANGUSTIAS). Go on!

ANGUSTIAS. For more than a week now Pepe's been leaving at one o'clock. God strike me dead if I'm lying.

MARTIRIO (*entering*). I heard him leaving at four o'clock too.

BERNARDA. But did you see him with your own eyes?

MARTIRIO. I didn't want to show myself. Don't you talk at the window facing the alley-way?

ANGUSTIAS. I talk to him from my bedroom window.

ADELA *appears at the door.*

MARTIRIO. Then . . .

BERNARDA. What is going on here?

PONCIA. Take care you don't discover the truth! But, obviously, Pepe was at one of the windows of your house at four in the morning.

BERNARDA. Are you quite certain?

PONCIA. Nothing in this life is known for certain.

ADELA. Mother, she wants to destroy us all. Don't listen to her!

BERNARDA. Then I shall find out for myself! If the villagers want to make false accusations, they'll find I'm as hard as flint. The matter is to be kept quiet. Sometimes there's a wave of filth which other people send to drown us.

MARTIRIO. I don't like lying.

PONCIA. There must be something in it.

BERNARDA. There is nothing. I was born with my eyes open. Now I shall keep them open until the day I die.

ANGUSTIAS. Yo tengo derecho de enterarme.

BERNARDA. Tú no tienes derecho más que a obedecer. Nadie me traiga ni me lleve. (*A* PONCIA.) Y tú te metes en los asuntos de tu casa. ¡Aquí no se vuelve a dar un paso que yo no sienta!

CRIADA (*entrando*). ¡En lo alto de la calle hay un gran gentío y todos los vecinos están en sus puertas!

BERNARDA (*a* PONCIA). ¡Corre a enterarte de lo que pasa! (*Las mujeres corren para salir.*) ¿Dónde vais? Siempre os supe mujeres ventaneras y rompedoras de su luto. ¡Vosotras al patio!

> *Salen y sale* BERNARDA. *Se oyen rumores lejanos. Entran* MARTIRIO *y* ADELA, *que se quedan escuchando y sin atreverse a dar un paso más de la puerta de salida.*

MARTIRIO. Agradece a la casualidad que no desaté mi lengua.

ADELA. También hubiera hablado yo.

MARTIRIO. ¿Y qué ibas a decir? ¡Querer no es hacer!

ADELA. Hace la que puede y la que se adelanta. Tú querías, pero no has podido.

MARTIRIO. No seguirás mucho tiempo.

ADELA. ¡Lo tendré todo!

MARTIRIO. Yo romperé tus abrazos.

ADELA (*suplicante*). ¡Martirio, déjame!

MARTIRIO. ¡De ninguna!

ADELA. ¡El me quiere para su casa!

MARTIRIO. ¡He visto cómo te abrazaba!

ADELA. Yo no quería. He ido como arrastrada por una maroma.

MARTIRIO. ¡Primero muerta!

> *Se asoman* MAGDALENA *y* ANGUSTIAS. *Se siente crecer el tumulto.*

ANGUSTIAS. I've a right to know what's going on.

BERNARDA. You have no right except to obey. No one tells me what to do. (*To* PONCIA.) You stick to your own affairs in your own house. No one will take a step in mine without my knowledge!

SERVANT (*entering*). There's a big crowd at the top of the street and all the neighbours are at their doors!

BERNARDA (*to* PONCIA). Go quickly! Find out what's happening! (*The women run as if to go out.*) Where are you going? I always knew you were girls for displaying yourselves at the windows. You can't wait to break your mourning. All of you to the courtyard!

> *They leave and* BERNARDA *leaves too. Distant sounds are heard.* MARTIRIO *and* ADELA *enter. They stand listening, not daring to take another step towards the door that leads out.*

MARTIRIO. Thank your lucky stars that I didn't speak up.

ADELA. I could have spoken up too.

MARTIRIO. And what were you going to say? Wanting and doing are not the same thing!

ADELA. The one who does is the one who can, the one who gets there first. You wanted to but you couldn't.

MARTIRIO. This can't go on much longer.

ADELA. I'll have him all for myself!

MARTIRIO. I'll pull your arms away from him!

ADELA (*pleading*). Martirio, leave me alone!

MARTIRIO. Never!

ADELA. He wants me to live with him.

MARTIRIO. I saw how he embraced you!

ADELA. I didn't want to. It's as if I was dragged by a rope.

MARTIRIO. I'll see you dead first!

> MAGDALENA *and* ANGUSTIAS *appear. The noise is heard growing louder.*

PONCIA (*entrando con* BERNARDA). ¡Bernarda!

BERNARDA. ¿Qué ocurre?

PONCIA. La hija de la Librada, la soltera, tuvo un hijo no se sabe con quién.

ADELA. ¿Un hijo?

PONCIA. Y para ocultar su vergüenza lo mató y lo metió debajo de unas piedras; pero unos perros, con más corazón que muchas criaturas, lo sacaron y como llevados por la mano de Dios lo han puesto en el tranco de su puerta. Ahora la quieren matar. La traen arrastrando por la calle abajo, y por las trochas y los terrenos del olivar vienen los hombres corriendo, dando unas voces que estremecen los campos.

BERNARDA. Sí, que vengan todos con varas de olivo y mangos de azadones, que vengan todos para matarla.

ADELA. ¡No, no, para matarla no!

MARTIRIO. Sí, y vamos a salir también nosotras.

BERNARDA. Y que pague la que pisotea su decencia.

Fuera se oye un grito de mujer y un gran rumor.

ADELA. ¡Que la dejen escapar! ¡No salgáis vosotras!

MARTIRIO (*mirando a* ADELA). ¡Que pague lo que debe!

BERNARDA (*bajo el arco*). ¡Acabar con ella antes que lleguen los guardias! ¡Carbón ardiendo en el sitio de su pecado!

ADELA (*cogiéndose el vientre*). ¡No! ¡No!

BERNARDA. ¡Matadla! ¡Matadla!

Telón.

PONCIA (*entering with* BERNARDA). Bernarda!

BERNARDA. What's happening?

PONCIA. Librada's daughter, the unmarried one, has had a child, and no one knows who by.

ADELA. A child?

PONCIA. And to hide her shame she killed it and buried it under some stones; but some dogs, with more heart than many a human being, rooted it out and, as if guided by the hand of God, left it on her doorstep. Now they want to kill her. They are dragging her down the street, and the men are running along the paths and from the olive-groves, shouting so loud they are making the fields tremble.

BERNARDA. Yes! Let them come with olive switches and pick-handles. Let them all come and kill her.

ADELA. No, no! Not kill her! No!

MARTIRIO. Yes! And let's go out there too!

BERNARDA. And let the woman who tramples on her decency pay the price.

Outside a woman's cry is heard and a great clamour.

ADELA. Let her go! Don't go out!

MARTIRIO (*looking at* ADELA). Let her pay the price!

BERNARDA (*in the archway*). Finish her off before the police arrive! A red-hot coal in the place of her sin!

ADELA (*clutching her stomach*). No, no!

BERNARDA. Kill her! Kill her!

Curtain.

Acto Tercero

Cuatro paredes blancas ligeramente azuladas del patio interior de la casa de BERNARDA. *Es de noche. El decorado ha de ser de una perfecta simplicidad. Las puertas, iluminadas por la luz de los interiores, dan un tenue fulgor a la escena. En el centro, una mesa con un quinqué, donde están comiendo* BERNARDA *y sus hijas. La* PONCIA *las sirve.* PRUDENCIA *está sentada aparte. Al levantarse el telón hay un gran silencio, interrumpido por el ruido de platos y cubiertos.*

PRUDENCIA. Ya me voy. Os he hecho una visita larga. (*Se levanta.*)

BERNARDA. Espérate, mujer. No nos vemos nunca.

PRUDENCIA. ¿Han dado el último toque para el rosario?

PONCIA. Todavía no.

> PRUDENCIA *se sienta.*

BERNARDA. ¿Y tu marido cómo sigue?

PRUDENCIA. Igual.

BERNARDA. Tampoco lo vemos.

PRUDENCIA. Ya sabes sus costumbres. Desde que se peleó con sus hermanos por la herencia no ha salido por la puerta de la calle. Pone una escalera y salta las tapias del corral.

BERNARDA. Es un verdadero hombre. ¿Y con tu hija? . . .

PRUDENCIA. No la ha perdonado.

BERNARDA. Hace bien.

PRUDENCIA. No sé qué te diga. Yo sufro por esto.

BERNARDA. Una hija que desobedece deja de ser hija para convertirse en enemiga.

Act Three

Four white walls, lightly bathed in blue, in the inner courtyard of BERNARDA's *house. It is night. The set should have a perfect simplicity. The doorways, illuminated by the light from inside the house, cast a delicate glow on the scene. Centre-stage a table with an oil-lamp at which* BERNARDA *and her daughters are eating.* PONCIA *is serving them.* PRUDENCIA *is sitting to one side. The curtain rises on total silence, broken only by the sound of plates and cutlery.*

PRUDENCIA. I must be going now. I've stayed too long as it is. (*She gets up.*)

BERNARDA. No need to rush, woman. We hardly ever see each other.

PRUDENCIA. Has the last call for the rosary sounded?

PONCIA. Not yet.

PRUDENCIA *sits down.*

BERNARDA. How is your husband these days?

PRUDENCIA. Just the same.

BERNARDA. We never see him either.

PRUDENCIA. You know what he's like. Since he quarrelled with his brothers over the inheritance, he hasn't gone out by the front door. He uses a ladder to climb the back wall.

BERNARDA. That's what I call a man! How is he with your daughter?

PRUDENCIA. He hasn't forgiven her.

BERNARDA. He's quite right.

PRUDENCIA. I don't know what to say. I suffer because of it.

BERNARDA. A disobedient daughter stops being a true daughter. She's more like an enemy.

PRUDENCIA. Yo dejo que el agua corra. No me queda más consuelo que refugiarme en la iglesia, pero como estoy quedando sin vista tendré que dejar de venir para que no jueguen con una los chiquillos. (*Se oye un gran golpe, como dado en los muros.*) ¿Qué es eso?

BERNARDA. El caballo garañón, que está encerrado y da coces contra el muro. (*A voces.*) ¡Trabadlo y que salga al corral! (*En voz baja.*) Debe tener calor.

PRUDENCIA. ¿Vais a echarle las potras nuevas?

BERNARDA. Al amanecer.

PRUDENCIA. Has sabido acrecentar tu ganado.

BERNARDA. A fuerza de dinero y sinsabores.

PONCIA (*interviniendo*). ¡Pero tiene la mejor manada de estos contornos! Es una lástima que esté bajo de precio.

BERNARDA. ¿Quieres un poco de queso y miel?

PRUDENCIA. Estoy desganada.

   Se oye otra vez el golpe.

PONCIA. ¡Por Dios!

PRUDENCIA. ¡Me ha retemblado dentro del pecho!

BERNARDA (*levantándose furiosa*). ¿Hay que decir las cosas dos veces? ¡Echadlo que se revuelque en los montones de paja! (*Pausa, y como hablando con los gañanes.*) Pues encerrad las potras en la cuadra, pero dejadlo libre, no sea que nos eche abajo las paredes. (*Se dirige a la mesa y se sienta otra vez.*) ¡Ay, qué vida!

PRUDENCIA. Bregando como un hombre.

BERNARDA. Así es.

   ADELA *se levanta de la mesa.*

¿Dónde vas?

PRUDENCIA. I let the water flow. The only comfort I have left is the church, but now that I'm going blind I'll have to stop going, so the children can't tease me.

A heavy blow is heard against the walls.

What's that?

BERNARDA. The stallion locked in the stable. He's kicking the wall. (*Loudly.*) Hobble him and let him out into the yard. (*In a normal voice.*) He must be hot.

PRUDENCIA. Are you going to let him loose on the new mares?

BERNARDA. At sunrise.

PRUDENCIA. You've known how to increase your stable.

BERNARDA. Thanks to money and lots of worry.

PONCIA (*breaking in*). She's got the best stable in the whole region. A pity the prices are low.

BERNARDA. Would you like some cheese and honey?

PRUDENCIA. I've no appetite.

The blow is heard again.

PONCIA. In God's name!

PRUDENCIA. My heart almost stopped!

BERNARDA (*rising angrily*). Do I have to say everything twice? Let him out to roll in the straw! (*Pause, and as though speaking to the farmhands.*) Lock the mares in the stable but let him loose, before he brings the walls on top of us.

She goes to the table and sits down again.

What a life this is!

PRUDENCIA. Struggling like a man.

BERNARDA. The way things are.

ADELA gets up from the table.

Where are you going?

ADELA. A beber agua.

BERNARDA (*en alta voz*). Trae un jarro de agua fresca. (*A* ADELA.) Puedes sentarte.

ADELA *se sienta.*

PRUDENCIA. Y Angustias, ¿cuándo se casa?

BERNARDA. Vienen a pedirla dentro de tres días.

PRUDENCIA. ¡Estarás contenta!

ANGUSTIAS. ¡Claro!

AMELIA (*a* MAGDALENA). ¡Ya has derramado la sal!

MAGDALENA. Peor suerte que tienes no vas a tener.

AMELIA. Siempre trae mala sombra.

BERNARDA. ¡Vamos!

PRUDENCIA (*a* ANGUSTIAS). ¿Te ha regalado ya el anillo?

ANGUSTIAS. Mírelo usted. (*Se lo alarga.*)

PRUDENCIA. Es precioso. Tres perlas. En mi tiempo las perlas significaban lágrimas.

ANGUSTIAS. Pero ya las cosas han cambiado.

ADELA. Yo creo que no. Las cosas significan siempre lo mismo. Los anillos de pedida deben ser de diamantes.

PRUDENCIA. Es más propio.

BERNARDA. Con perlas o sin ellas las cosas son como una se las propone.

MARTIRIO. O como Dios dispone.

PRUDENCIA. Los muebles me han dicho que son preciosos.

BERNARDA. Dieciséis mil reales he gastado.

PONCIA (*interviniendo*). Lo mejor es el armario de luna.

PRUDENCIA. Nunca vi un mueble de éstos.

BERNARDA. Nosotras tuvimos arca.

PRUDENCIA. Lo preciso es que todo sea para bien.

ADELA. Que nunca se sabe.

ADELA. For a drink of water.

BERNARDA (*calling out*). Bring a jug of cold water. (*To* ADELA.) Sit down.

ADELA *sits down.*

PRUDENCIA. And Angustias, when is she getting married?

BERNARDA. They'll be coming to make a formal request in the next three days.

PRUDENCIA. You must be pleased!

ANGUSTIAS. Of course!

AMELIA (*to* MAGDALENA). Now you've spilled the salt.

MAGDALENA. Your luck can't get worse than it is already.

AMELIA. It always brings bad luck.

BERNARDA. Enough of that!

PRUDENCIA (*to* ANGUSTIAS). Has he given you the ring yet?

ANGUSTIAS. Take a look. (*She holds it out.*)

PRUDENCIA. It's beautiful. Three pearls. In my time pearls meant tears.

ANGUSTIAS. But things have changed now.

ADELA. Oh, I don't think so. Things always mean the same. Engagement rings ought to have diamonds.

PRUDENCIA. It is more appropriate.

BERNARDA. With pearls or without them, things are what we make them.

MARTIRIO. Or as God wills them!

PRUDENCIA. They tell me your furniture is beautiful.

BERNARDA. I spent sixteen thousand *reales*.

PONCIA (*breaking in*). The best piece is the wardrobe with the mirror.

PRUDENCIA. I've never seen one of those.

BERNARDA. All we had was a chest.

PRUDENCIA. What matters is that everything works out for the best.

ADELA. You can never tell.

BERNARDA. No hay motivo para que no lo sea.

Se oyen lejanísimas unas campanas.

PRUDENCIA. El último toque. (*A* ANGUSTIAS.) Ya vendré a que me enseñes la ropa.

ANGUSTIAS. Cuando usted quiera.

PRUDENCIA. Buenas noches nos dé Dios.

BERNARDA. Adiós, Prudencia.

LAS CINCO (*a la vez*). Vaya usted con Dios.

Pausa. Sale PRUDENCIA.

BERNARDA. Ya hemos comido.

Se levantan.

ADELA. Voy a llegarme hasta el portón para estirar las piernas y tomar un poco el fresco.

MAGDALENA *se sienta en una silla baja retrepada contra la pared.*

AMELIA. Yo voy contigo.

MARTIRIO. Y yo.

ADELA (*con odio contenido*). No me voy a perder.

AMELIA. La noche quiere compaña.

Salen. BERNARDA *se sienta y* ANGUSTIAS *está arreglando la mesa.*

BERNARDA. Ya te he dicho que quiero que hables con tu hermana Martirio. Lo que pasó del retrato fue una broma y lo debes olvidar.

ANGUSTIAS. Usted sabe que ella no me quiere.

BERNARDA. Cada uno sabe lo que piensa por dentro. Yo no me meto en los corazones, pero quiero buena fachada y armonía familiar. ¿Lo entiendes?

ANGUSTIAS. Sí.

BERNARDA. There's no reason why it shouldn't.

Bells are heard in the distance.

PRUDENCIA. The last call. (*To* ANGUSTIAS.) I'll come again so you can show me your trousseau.

ANGUSTIAS. Whenever you like.

PRUDENCIA. May God be with us all tonight.

BERNARDA. Goodbye, Prudencia.

THE FIVE GIRLS (*together*). God go with you.

Pause. PRUDENCIA *leaves.*

BERNARDA. You may leave the table.

They get up.

ADELA. I'm going as far as the main door to stretch my legs and get some air.

MAGDALENA *sits down on a low chair against the wall.*

AMELIA. I'll come with you.

MARTIRIO. Me too.

ADELA (*with contained hatred*). I'm not going to get lost.

AMELIA. You should have company at night.

They leave. BERNARDA *sits.* ANGUSTIAS *is clearing the table.*

BERNARDA. I've told you already I want you to talk to Martirio. What happened with the picture was a joke. You should forget it.

ANGUSTIAS. You know she doesn't love me.

BERNARDA. What we feel inside is our own affair. I never pry into anyone's heart, but I want a respectable appearance, and harmony inside the family. Do you understand?

ANGUSTIAS. Yes.

BERNARDA. Pues ya está.

MAGDALENA (*casi dormida*). Además, ¡si te vas a ir antes de nada! (*Se duerme.*)

ANGUSTIAS. Tarde me parece.

BERNARDA. ¿A qué hora terminaste anoche de hablar?

ANGUSTIAS. A las doce y media.

BERNARDA. ¿Qué cuenta Pepe?

ANGUSTIAS. Yo lo encuentro distraído. Me habla siempre como pensando en otra cosa. Si le pregunto qué le pasa, me contesta: 'Los hombres tenemos nuestras preocupaciones.'

BERNARDA. No le debes preguntar. Y cuando te cases, menos. Habla si él habla y míralo cuando te mire. Así no tendrás disgustos.

ANGUSTIAS. Yo creo, madre, que él me oculta muchas cosas.

BERNARDA. No procures descubrirlas, no le preguntes y, desde luego, que no te vea llorar jamás.

ANGUSTIAS. Debía estar contenta y no lo estoy.

BERNARDA. Eso es lo mismo.

ANGUSTIAS. Muchas veces miro a Pepe con mucha fijeza y se me borra a través de los hierros, como si lo tapara una nube de polvo de las que levantan los rebaños.

BERNARDA. Eso son cosas de debilidad.

ANGUSTIAS. ¡Ojalá!

BERNARDA. ¿Viene esta noche?

ANGUSTIAS. No. Fue con su madre a la capital.

BERNARDA. Así nos acostaremos antes. ¡Magdalena!

ANGUSTIAS. Está dormida.

Entran ADELA, MARTIRIO *y* AMELIA.

AMELIA. ¡Qué noche más oscura!

ADELA. No se ve a dos pasos de distancia.

MARTIRIO. Una buena noche para ladrones, para el que necesite escondrijo.

BERNARDA. Then that's settled.

MAGDALENA (*half asleep*). Anyway, you'll be leaving soon.

She falls alseep.

ANGUSTIAS. Not soon enough for me!

BERNARDA. What time did you stop talking last night?

ANGUSTIAS. Half-past twelve.

BERNARDA. What does Pepe have to say?

ANGUSTIAS. I find him distracted. He always talks to me as if his mind is on something else. If I ask him what's wrong, he says: 'We men have our problems.'

BERNARDA. You shouldn't ask him. And when you marry, less still. Speak if he speaks and look at him when he looks at you. Do that and you won't have disagreements.

ANGUSTIAS. Mother, I think he's hiding things from me.

BERNARDA. Don't try to find out what they are. Don't ask him, and, above all, never let him see you cry.

ANGUSTIAS. I ought to be happy but I'm not.

BERNARDA. It's all the same.

ANGUSTIAS. I often look at Pepe hard and he becomes blurred through the bars, as if he were hidden in a cloud of dust stirred up by flocks of sheep.

BERNARDA. It's because you aren't strong.

ANGUSTIAS. I hope it's just that.

BERNARDA. Is he coming tonight?

ANGUSTIAS. No. He's gone to the city with his mother.

BERNARDA. Then we'll have an early night. Magdalena!

ANGUSTIAS. She's fallen asleep.

ADELA, MARTIRIO *and* AMELIA *enter.*

AMELIA. It's pitch black outside!

ADELA. You can't see your hand in front of your face.

MARTIRIO. A good night for thieves, for someone who needs to hide.

ADELA. El caballo garañón estaba en el centro del corral.
¡Blanco! Doble de grande, llenando todo lo oscuro.

AMELIA. Es verdad. Daba miedo. ¡Parecía una aparición!

ADELA. Tiene el cielo unas estrellas como puños.

MARTIRIO. Esta se puso a mirarlas de modo que se iba a
tronchar el cuello.

ADELA. ¿Es que no te gustan a ti?

MARTIRIO. A mí las cosas de tejas arriba no me importan
nada. Con lo que pasa dentro de las habitaciones tengo
bastante.

ADELA. Así te va a ti.

BERNARDA. A ella le va en lo suyo como a ti en lo tuyo.

ANGUSTIAS. Buenas noches.

ADELA. ¿Ya te acuestas?

ANGUSTIAS. Sí, esta noche no viene Pepe. (*Sale.*)

ADELA. Madre, ¿por qué cuando se corre una estrella o
luce un relámpago se dice:
   Santa Bárbara bendita,
   que en el cielo estás escrita
   con papel y agua bendita?

BERNARDA. Los antiguos sabían muchas cosas que hemos
olvidado.

AMELIA. Yo cierro los ojos para no verlas.

ADELA. Yo no. A mí me gusta ver correr lleno de lumbre
lo que está quieto y quieto años enteros.

MARTIRIO. Pero estas cosas nada tienen que ver con
nosotros.

BERNARDA. Y es mejor no pensar en ellas.

ADELA. ¡Qué noche más hermosa! Me gustaría quedarme
hasta muy tarde para disfrutar el fresco del campo.

BERNARDA. Pero hay que acostarse. ¡Magdalena!

AMELIA. Está en el primer sueño.

BERNARDA. ¡Magdalena!

MAGDALENA (*disgustada*). ¡Dejarme en paz!

BERNARDA. ¡A la cama!

ADELA. The stallion was in the middle of the yard. Pure white! And twice its size, filling the darkness.

AMELIA. It's true. It was frightening. He was like a ghost!

ADELA. There are stars in the sky as big as fists.

MARTIRIO. She was staring at them so much she almost cricked her neck.

ADELA. Don't you enjoy looking at them?

MARTIRIO. I couldn't care less what happens above the rooftops. I've enough on my plate with what goes on inside these rooms.

ADELA. You are that kind of person.

BERNARDA. She has her ways and you have yours.

ANGUSTIAS. Good night.

ADELA. Going to bed already?

ANGUSTIAS. Yes. Pepe's not coming tonight. (*She goes out.*)

ADELA. Mother, when there's a shooting star or a flash of lightning, why do we say: 'Blessed Santa Barbara, you are written in the sky with paper and holy water'?

BERNARDA. The ancients knew many things that we have forgotten.

AMELIA. I close my eyes so as not to see them.

ADELA. Not me. I like to see things flash with fire when they've been asleep for years on end.

MARTIRIO. Such things have nothing to do with us.

BERNARDA. It's better not to think of them.

ADELA. Such a beautiful night! I'd love to stay up late to enjoy the breeze from the fields.

BERNARDA. But it's time for bed. Magdalena!

AMELIA. She's dozed off.

BERNARDA. Magdalena!

MAGDALENA (*annoyed*). Leave me in peace!

BERNARDA. Get to bed!

MAGDALENA (*levantándose malhumorada*). ¡No la dejáis a una tranquila! (*Se va refunfuñando.*)

AMELIA. Buenas noches. (*Se va.*)

BERNARDA. Andar vosotras también.

MARTIRIO. ¿Cómo es que esta noche no viene el novio de Angustias?

BERNARDA. Fue de viaje.

MARTIRIO (*mirando a* ADELA). ¡Ah!

ADELA. Hasta mañana. (*Sale.*)

> MARTIRIO *bebe agua y sale lentamente mirando hacia la puerta del corral. Sale la* PONCIA.

PONCIA. ¿Estás todavía aquí?

BERNARDA. Disfrutando este silencio y sin lograr ver por parte alguna 'la cosa tan grande' que aquí pasa, según tú.

PONCIA. Bernarda, dejemos esa conversación.

BERNARDA. En esta casa no hay un sí ni un no. Mi vigilancia lo puede todo.

PONCIA. No pasa nada por fuera. Eso es verdad. Tus hijas están y viven como metidas en alacenas. Pero ni tú ni nadie puede vigilar por el interior de los pechos.

BERNARDA. Mis hijas tienen la respiración tranquila.

PONCIA. Eso te importa a ti que eres su madre. A mí, con servir tu casa tengo bastante.

BERNARDA. Ahora te has vuelto callada.

PONCIA. Me estoy en mi sitio y en paz.

BERNARDA. Lo que pasa es que no tienes nada que decir. Si en esta casa hubiera hierbas, ya te encargarías de traer a pastar las ovejas del vecindario.

PONCIA. Yo tapo más de lo que te figuras.

BERNARDA. ¿Sigue tu hijo viendo a Pepe a las cuatro de la mañana? ¿Siguen diciendo todavía la mala letanía de esta casa?

PONCIA. No dicen nada.

MAGDALENA (*getting up, in a bad mood*). You never let a person be! (*She goes out grumbling.*)

AMELIA. Good night. (*She leaves.*)

BERNARDA. You go too.

MARTIRIO. Why isn't Angustias' fiancé coming tonight?

BERNARDA. He's gone on a visit.

MARTIRIO (*looking at* ADELA). Ah!

ADELA. See you in the morning. (*She goes out.*)

> MARTIRIO *takes a drink of water and goes out slowly, looking towards the door to the stable-yard.* PONCIA *enters.*

PONCIA. Still here?

BERNARDA. Enjoying the silence and not seeing the 'something serious' that's happening here, according to you.

PONCIA. Bernarda, let's not talk about that.

BERNARDA. In this house there's nothing going on that my watchfulness can't cope with.

PONCIA. Nothing on the outside, true. Your daughters live as if they were kept in a cupboard. But neither you nor anyone else can see inside their hearts.

BERNARDA. My daughters breathe easily.

PONCIA. That's important to you, as their mother. As for me, I've enough to do looking after your house.

BERNARDA. You've gone very quiet.

PONCIA. I know my place. That's all there is to it.

BERNARDA. The truth is you've got nothing to say. If there were grass in this house, you'd make it your business to bring the neighbourhood's sheep to graze.

PONCIA. I cover up more than you think.

BERNARDA. Does your son still see Pepe at four in the morning? Are they still reciting their litany of lies about this house?

PONCIA. They don't say anything.

BERNARDA. Porque no pueden. Porque no hay carne donde morder. ¡A la vigilia de mis ojos se debe esto!

PONCIA. Bernarda, yo no quiero hablar porque temo tus intenciones. Pero no estés segura.

BERNARDA. ¡Segurísima!

PONCIA. ¡A lo mejor de pronto cae un rayo! A lo mejor, de pronto, un golpe de sangre te para el corazón.

BERNARDA. Aquí no pasará nada. Ya estoy alerta contra tus suposiciones.

PONCIA. Pues mejor para ti.

BERNARDA. ¡No faltaba más!

CRIADA (*entrando*). Ya terminé de fregar los platos. ¿Manda usted algo, Bernarda?

BERNARDA (*levantándose*). Nada. Yo voy a descansar.

PONCIA. ¿A qué hora quiere que la llame?

BERNARDA. A ninguna. Esta noche voy a dormir bien. (*Se va.*)

PONCIA. Cuando una no puede con el mar lo más fácil es volver las espaldas para no verlo.

CRIADA. Es tan orgullosa que ella misma se pone una venda en los ojos.

PONCIA. Yo no puedo hacer nada. Quise atajar las cosas, pero ya me asustan demasiado. ¿Tú ves este silencio? Pues hay una tormenta en cada cuarto. El día que estallen nos barrerán a todas. Yo he dicho lo que tenía que decir.

CRIADA. Bernarda cree que nadie puede con ella y no sabe la fuerza que tiene un hombre entre mujeres solas.

PONCIA. No es toda la culpa de Pepe el Romano. Es verdad que el año pasado anduvo detrás de Adela, y ésta estaba loca por él, pero ella debió estarse en su sitio y no provocarlo. Un hombre es un hombre.

CRIADA. Hay quien cree que habló muchas noches con Adela.

PONCIA. Es verdad. (*En voz baja.*) Y otras cosas.

BERNARDA. Because they can't. Because there is no meat to bite on. And that's because of my vigilance.

PONCIA. Bernarda, I don't want to talk because I'm afraid of the things you are always hinting at. But don't be too sure.

BERNARDA. I'm very sure!

PONCIA. Lightning strikes suddenly! A clot of blood could stop your heart.

BERNARDA. Nothing will happen here! I know what you're insinuating. I'm on my guard.

PONCIA. I hope so, for your sake.

BERNARDA. I most certainly am!

SERVANT (*entering*). I've finished the washing-up. Is there anything else, Bernarda?

BERNARDA (*getting up*). Nothing. I'm going to bed.

PONCIA. What time do you want me to call you?

BERNARDA. Don't. Tonight I'm going to sleep well. (*She goes out.*)

PONCIA. When you can't control the tide, the easiest thing is to turn your back so as not to see it.

SERVANT. She's so proud, she puts a blindfold over her eyes.

PONCIA. I can't do anything. I tried to head things off, but now they frighten me too much. Listen to this silence. There's a storm in every room. The day they break, they'll sweep us all away. I've said what I had to.

SERVANT. Bernarda thinks that no one can be a match for her. She doesn't know the power of a man over the hearts of lonely women.

PONCIA. It's not all Pepe el Romano's fault. It's true that last year he was after Adela and she was mad about him. But it was her place not to lead him on. A man is a man.

SERVANT. They say he spoke to Adela many a night.

PONCIA. It's true. (*Lowering her voice.*) And other things.

CRIADA. No sé lo que va a pasar aquí.

PONCIA. A mí me gustaría cruzar el mar y dejar esta casa de guerra.

CRIADA. Bernarda está aligerando la boda y es posible que nada pase.

PONCIA. Las cosas se han puesto ya demasiado maduras. Adela está decidida a lo que sea, y las demás vigilan sin descanso.

CRIADA. ¿Y Martirio también? . . .

PONCIA. Esa es la peor. Es un pozo de veneno. Ve que el Romano no es para ella y hundiría el mundo si estuviera en su mano.

CRIADA. ¡Es que son malas!

PONCIA. Son mujeres sin hombre, nada más. En estas cuestiones se olvida hasta la sangre. ¡Chisssssss! (*Escucha.*)

CRIADA. ¿Qué pasa?

PONCIA (*se levanta*). Están ladrando los perros.

CRIADA. Debe haber pasado alguien por el portón.

Sale ADELA *en enaguas blancas y corpiño.*

PONCIA. ¿No te habías acostado?

ADELA. Voy a beber agua. (*Bebe en un vaso de la mesa.*)

PONCIA. Yo te suponía dormida.

ADELA. Me despertó la sed. ¿Y vosotras no descansáis?

CRIADA. Ahora.

Sale ADELA.

PONCIA. Vámonos.

CRIADA. Ganado tenemos el sueño. Bernarda no me deja descanso en todo el día.

PONCIA. Llévate la luz.

CRIADA. Los perros están como locos.

SERVANT. I don't know what's going to happen here.

PONCIA. I'd like to cross the sea and leave this battlefield behind me.

SERVANT. Bernarda's rushing the wedding, so perhaps nothing will happen.

PONCIA. Things have already gone too far. Adela's mind is made up, no matter what, and the rest of them are watching all the time.

SERVANT. Martirio too?

PONCIA. She's the worst of all. She's a well of poison. She can see that Romano's not for her and she'd sink the world if she could.

SERVANT. They are all evil!

PONCIA. They are women without men, it's as simple as that. Even blood ties are forgotten then. Shhhh! (*She listens.*)

SERVANT. What is it?

PONCIA (*getting up*). The dogs are barking.

SERVANT. Someone must have passed the front door.

ADELA *enters in a white petticoat and bodice.*

PONCIA. I thought you'd gone to bed.

ADELA. I'm going to get a drink of water. (*She drinks from a glass on the table.*)

PONCIA. I thought you were asleep by now.

ADELA. I was so thirsty I woke up. Aren't you two going to bed?

SERVANT. In a minute.

ADELA *goes out.*

PONCIA. Let's go.

SERVANT. We've earned our rest. Bernarda keeps me at it all day long.

PONCIA. Take the lamp.

SERVANT. It's as if the dogs have gone mad.

PONCIA. No nos van a dejar dormir.

> *Salen. La escena queda casi a oscuras. Sale* MARÍA
> JOSEFA *con una oveja en los brazos.*

MARÍA JOSEFA.
Ovejita, niño mío,
vámonos a la orilla del mar.
La hormiguita estará en su puerta,
yo te daré la teta y el pan.

Bernarda, cara de leoparda.
Magdalena, cara de hiena.
Ovejita.
Meee, meee.
Vamos a los ramos del portal de Belén. (*Ríe.*)

Ni tú ni yo queremos dormir.
La puerta sola se abrirá
y en la playa nos meteremos
en una choza de coral.

Bernarda, cara de leoparda.
Magdalena, cara de hiena.
Ovejita.
Meee, meee.
¡Vamos a los ramos del portal de Belén!

> *Se va cantando. Entra* ADELA. *Mira a un lado y otro*
> *con sigilo, y desaparece por la puerta del corral. Sale*
> MARTIRIO *por otra puerta y queda en angustioso*
> *acecho en el centro de la escena. También va en*
> *enaguas. Se cubre con pequeño mantón negro de*
> *talle. Sale por enfrente de ella* MARÍA JOSEFA.

MARTIRIO. ¿Abuela, dónde va usted?
MARÍA JOSEFA. ¿Vas a abrirme la puerta? ¿Quién eres tú?

PONCIA. They'll keep us awake the entire night.

They leave. The stage is almost in darkness. MARÍA
JOSEFA *appears with a lamb in her arms.*

MARÍA JOSEFA.
Little lamb, my baby,
Let's go down to the seashore.
The little ant will be at his door.
I'll give you my breast and bread.

Bernarda, leopard face.
Magdalena, hyena face.
Little lamb.
Baa-baa-baa.
We'll go to the flowers at Bethlehem's gates. (*Laughs.*)

Nor you nor I now want to sleep.
We'll go in through the open door
And hide ourselves down on the shore
In a cabin made of coral.

Bernarda, leopard face.
Magdalena, hyena face.
Little lamb.
Baa-baa-baa.
We'll go to the flowers at Bethlehem's gates.

She goes out, singing. ADELA *enters. She looks
around cautiously and disappears through the door
to the stable-yard.* MARTIRIO *comes in by another
door and stands centre-stage in a state of anguished
watchfulness. She is also in her petticoat. She has
covered herself with a small black shawl down to her
waist.* MARÍA JOSEFA *enters from the opposite side.*

MARTIRIO. Grandmother, where are you going?
MARÍA JOSEFA. Will you open the door for me? Who are
you?

MARTIRIO. ¿Cómo está aquí?

MARÍA JOSEFA. Me escapé. ¿Tú quién eres?

MARTIRIO. Vaya a acostarse.

MARÍA JOSEFA. Tú eres Martirio, ya te veo. Martirio: cara de martirio. ¿Y cuándo vas a tener un niño? Yo he tenido éste.

MARTIRIO. ¿Dónde cogió esa oveja?

MARÍA JOSEFA. Ya sé que es una oveja. Pero, ¿por qué una oveja no va a ser un niño? Mejor es tener una oveja que no tener nada. Bernarda, cara de leoparda. Magdalena, cara de hiena.

MARTIRIO. No dé voces.

MARÍA JOSEFA. Es verdad. Está todo muy oscuro. Como tengo el pelo blanco crees que no puedo tener crías, y sí: crías y crías y crías. Este niño tendrá el pelo blanco y tendrá otro niño, y éste otro, y todos con el pelo de nieve seremos como las olas: una y otra y otra. Luego nos sentaremos todos, y todos tendremos el cabello blanco y seremos espuma. ¿Por qué aquí no hay espuma? Aquí no hay más que mantos de luto.

MARTIRIO. Calle, calle.

MARÍA JOSEFA. Cuando mi vecina tenía un niño yo le llevaba chocolate y luego ella me lo traía a mí, y así siempre, siempre, siempre. Tú tendrás el pelo blanco, pero no vendrán las vecinas. Yo tengo que marcharme, pero tengo miedo de que los perros me muerdan. ¿Me acompañarás tú a salir del campo? Yo no quiero campo. Yo quiero casas, pero casas abiertas, y las vecinas acostadas en sus camas con sus niños chiquitos, y los hombres fuera, sentados en sus sillas. Pepe el Romano es un gigante. Todas lo queréis. Pero él os va a devorar, porque vosotras sois granos de trigo. No granos de trigo, no. ¡Ranas sin lengua!

MARTIRIO (enérgica). Vamos, váyase a la cama. (La empuja.)

MARTIRIO. What are you doing here?

MARÍA JOSEFA. I escaped. Who are you?

MARTIRIO. Go back to bed.

MARÍA JOSEFA. You are Martirio, now I see you. Martirio: face of a martyr. When are you going to have a child? I've had this one.

MARTIRIO. Where did you get that lamb?

MARÍA JOSEFA. I know it's a lamb. But why can't a lamb be a child? It's better to have a lamb than nothing. Bernarda, leopard face. Magdalena, hyena face.

MARTIRIO. Keep your voice down!

MARÍA JOSEFA. It's true. Everything is so dark. Because my hair is white, you think I can't have children. And I can . . . children, and children and more children. This child will have white hair, and will have another child, and this one another one, and all of us, with our hair like snow, will be like the waves, one after another, after another. Then we'll all sit down, and all of us will have white hair, and we shall be foam. Why is there no foam here? Here there is nothing but shawls for mourning.

MARTIRIO. Be quiet, be quiet!

MARÍA JOSEFA. When my neighbour had a child, I used to take her chocolate, and then she would bring me some, and so it was, always, always, always. You'll have white hair, but the neighbours won't come. I have to go, but I'm afraid the dogs might bite me. Will you come with me till I'm past the fields? I don't want fields. I want houses, but open houses, and the women asleep in their beds with their little ones, and the men outside sitting in their chairs. Pepe el Romano is a giant. You all want him. But he will devour you all because you are grains of wheat. No, not grains of wheat. Frogs without tongues!

MARTIRIO (strongly). Come on! Go to bed! (She pushes her.)

MARÍA JOSEFA. Sí, pero luego tú me abrirás, ¿verdad?

MARTIRIO. De seguro.

MARÍA JOSEFA (*llorando*).

Ovejita, niño mío,
vámonos a la orilla del mar.
La hormiguita estará en su puerta,
yo te daré la teta y el pan.

> *Sale.* MARTIRIO *cierra la puerta por donde ha salido*
> MARÍA JOSEFA *y se dirige a la puerta del corral. Allí*
> *vacila, pero avanza dos pasos más.*

MARTIRIO (*en voz baja*). Adela. (*Pausa. Avanza hasta la misma puerta. En voz alta.*) ¡Adela!

> *Aparece* ADELA. *Viene un poco despeinada.*

ADELA. ¿Por qué me buscas?

MARTIRIO. ¡Deja a ese hombre!

ADELA. ¿Quién eres tú para decírmelo?

MARTIRIO. No es ése el sitio de una mujer honrada.

ADELA. ¡Con qué ganas te has quedado de ocuparlo!

MARTIRIO (*en voz alta*). Ha llegado el momento de que yo hable. Esto no puede seguir.

ADELA. Esto no es más que el comienzo. He tenido fuerza para adelantarme. El brío y el mérito que tú no tienes. He visto la muerte debajo de estos techos y he salido a buscar lo que era mío, lo que me pertenecía.

MARTIRIO. Ese hombre sin alma vino por otra. Tú te has atravesado.

ADELA. Vino por el dinero, pero sus ojos los puso siempre en mí.

MARTIRIO. Yo no permitiré que lo arrebates. El se casará con Angustias.

ADELA. Sabes mejor que yo que no la quiere.

MARÍA JOSEFA. All right, but then you'll let me out, won't you?

MARTIRIO. Of course.

MARÍA JOSEFA (*weeping*).

Little lamb, my baby,
Let's go down to the seashore.
The little ant will be at his door.
I'll give you my breast and bread.

> *She leaves.* MARTIRIO *closes the door through which* MARÍA JOSEFA *has just gone out and moves towards the door to the stable-yard. There she hesitates before taking two more steps.*

MARTIRIO (*quietly*). Adela! (*She pauses, advances to the door. Loudly.*) Adela!

> ADELA *appears. Her hair is a little dishevelled.*

ADELA. Why are you looking for me?

MARTIRIO. Stay away from that man!

ADELA. Who are you to tell me that?

MARTIRIO. That's not the place for a decent woman!

ADELA. Wouldn't you like to be there yourself!

MARTIRIO (*loudly*). The time has come for me to speak out. This can't go on!

ADELA. This is just the beginning. I've had the strength to take what I want. The spirit and the looks that you don't have. I've seen death under this roof and so I went out to get what was mine, what belonged to me.

MARTIRIO. That man has no heart. He came for another woman. You've come between them.

ADELA. He came for the money, but his eyes were always on me!

MARTIRIO. I won't let you take him! He shall marry Angustias!

ADELA. You know as well as I do that he doesn't love her.

MARTIRIO. Lo sé.

ADELA. Sabes, porque lo has visto, que me quiere a mí.

MARTIRIO (*desesperada*). Sí.

ADELA (*acercándose*). Me quiere a mí, me quiere a mí.

MARTIRIO. Clávame un cuchillo si es tu gusto, pero no me lo digas más.

ADELA. Por eso procuras que no vaya con él. No te importa que abrace a la que no quiere. A mí tampoco. Ya puede estar cien años con Angustias. Pero que me abrace a mí se te hace terrible, porque tú lo quieres también, ¡lo quieres!

MARTIRIO (*dramática*). ¡Sí! Déjame decirlo con la cabeza fuera de los embozos. ¡Sí! Déjame que el pecho se me rompa como una granada de amargura. ¡Lo quiero!

ADELA (*en un arranque, y abrazándola*). Martirio, Martirio, yo no tengo la culpa.

MARTIRIO. ¡No me abraces! No quieras ablandar mis ojos. Mi sangre ya no es la tuya, y aunque quisiera verte como hermana no te miro ya más que como mujer. (*La rechaza.*)

ADELA. Aquí no hay ningún remedio. La que tenga que ahogarse que se ahogue. Pepe el Romano es mío. El me lleva a los juncos de la orilla.

MARTIRIO. ¡No será!

ADELA. Ya no aguanto el horror de estos techos después de haber probado el sabor de su boca. Seré lo que él quiera que sea. Todo el pueblo contra mí, quemándome con sus dedos de lumbre, perseguida por los que dicen que son decentes, y me pondré delante de todos la corona de espinas que tienen las que son queridas de algún hombre casado.

MARTIRIO. ¡Calla!

ADELA. Sí, sí. (*En voz baja.*) Vamos a dormir, vamos a dejar que se case con Angustias. Ya no me importa. Pero

MARTIRIO. I know.

ADELA. You know, because you've seen it, that he loves *me*!

MARTIRIO (*desperately*). Yes.

ADELA (*coming closer*). He loves *me*! He loves *me*!

MARTIRIO. Put a knife in me if you like, but don't say that again!

ADELA. That's why you want to stop me going with him. You don't care if he goes with a woman he doesn't love. Neither do I! He can spend a hundred years with Angustias. But for him to embrace me is something you can't stand, because you love him too. You love him!

MARTIRIO (*powerfully*). Yes! Why should I hide my head in shame? Let my bitter heart burst open like a pomegranate! I love him!

ADELA (*impulsively, going to embrace her*). Martirio, Martirio, I'm not to blame.

MARTIRIO. Don't touch me! Don't try to soften the hatred in my eyes! My blood is no longer yours. I want to see you as my sister, but I can only see you as a woman. (*She pushes her away*.)

ADELA. There's no solution here. Whoever must drown, must drown. Pepe el Romano's mine. He'll take me to the rushes at the edge of the water.

MARTIRIO. I won't let it happen!

ADELA. I can't stand the horror of this house any more, not after knowing the taste of his mouth. I'll be whatever he wants me to be. The whole village against me, burning me with their fingers of fire, hounded by those who claim they are respectable, and in front of them all I'll put on the crown of thorns that women wear who are loved by a married man.

MARTIRIO. Be quiet!

ADELA. Yes, yes. (*Quietly.*) Let's go to sleep. We'll let him marry Angustias. I don't care any more. But I'll go to a

yo me iré a una casita sola donde él me verá cuando quiera, cuando le venga en gana.

MARTIRIO. Eso no pasará mientras yo tenga una gota de sangre en el cuerpo.

ADELA. No a ti, que eres débil: a un caballo encabritado soy capaz de poner de rodillas con la fuerza de mi dedo meñique.

MARTIRIO. No levantes esa voz que me irrita. Tengo el corazón lleno de una fuerza tan mala, que, sin quererlo yo, a mí misma me ahoga.

ADELA. Nos enseñan a querer a las hermanas. Dios me ha debido dejar sola, en medio de la oscuridad, porque te veo como si no te hubiera visto nunca.

Se oye un silbido y ADELA *corre a la puerta, pero* MARTIRIO *se le pone delante.*

MARTIRIO. ¿Dónde vas?

ADELA. ¡Quítate de la puerta!

MARTIRIO. ¡Pasa si puedes!

ADELA. ¡Aparta! (*Lucha.*)

MARTIRIO (*a voces*). ¡Madre, madre!

ADELA. ¡Déjame!

Aparece BERNARDA. *Sale en enaguas con un mantón negro.*

BERNARDA. Quietas, quietas. ¡Qué pobreza la mía, no poder tener un rayo entre los dedos!

MARTIRIO (*señalando a* ADELA). ¡Estaba con él! ¡Mira esas enaguas llenas de paja de trigo!

BERNARDA. ¡Esa es la cama de las mal nacidas! (*Se dirige furiosa hacia* ADELA.)

ADELA (*haciéndole frente*). ¡Aquí se acabaron las voces de presidio! (ADELA *arrebata un bastón a su madre y lo parte en dos.*) Esto hago yo con la vara de la domina-

little house, alone, where he can see me whenever he wants, when the need comes upon him.

MARTIRIO. It shan't happen as long as I have a drop of blood in my veins.

ADELA. You won't stop me. You are far too weak. I can bring a wild stallion to its knees with the strength of my little finger.

MARTIRIO. Don't raise your voice. It grates on me. My heart is full of an evil force. In spite of myself, it's drowning me.

ADELA. They teach us to love our sisters. God must have abandoned me in the heart of darkness, because I'm seeing you as if I had never seen you before.

A whistle is heard and ADELA *runs to the door, but* MARTIRIO *steps in front of her.*

MARTIRIO. Where are you going?

ADELA. Get away from the door!

MARTIRIO. Get past if you can!

ADELA. Get away! (*She struggles.*)

MARTIRIO (*calling out*). Mother, Mother!

ADELA. Let me pass!

BERNARDA *appears. She enters in petticoats and a black shawl.*

BERNARDA. Behave! Behave! Quiet! If only I had a thunderbolt between my fingers!

MARTIRIO (*pointing at* ADELA). She was with him! Look at her petticoat, full of straw!

BERNARDA. The bed of whores! (*She angrily approaches* ADELA.)

ADELA (*confronting her*). An end to all your shouting! You aren't my jailer any more! (*She seizes her mother's stick and breaks it in two.*) That's what I do with the

dora. No dé usted un paso más. ¡En mí no manda nadie más que Pepe!

Sale MAGDALENA.

MAGDALENA. ¡Adela!

Salen la PONCIA *y* ANGUSTIAS.

ADELA. Yo soy su mujer. (*A* ANGUSTIAS.) Entérate tú y ve al corral a decírselo. El dominará toda esta casa. Ahí fuera está, respirando como si fuera un león.

ANGUSTIAS. ¡Dios mío!

BERNARDA. ¡La escopeta! ¿Dónde está la escopeta? (*Sale corriendo.*)

Aparece AMELIA *por el fondo, que mira aterrada, con la cabeza sobre la pared. Sale detrás* MARTIRIO.

ADELA. ¡Nadie podrá conmigo! (*Va a salir.*)

ANGUSTIAS (*sujetándola*). De aquí no sales con tu cuerpo en triunfo, ¡ladrona! ¡deshonra de nuestra casa!

MAGDALENA. ¡Déjala que se vaya donde no la veamos nunca más!

Suena un disparo.

BERNARDA (*entrando*). Atrévete a buscarlo ahora.

MARTIRIO (*entrando*). Se acabó Pepe el Romano.

ADELA. ¡Pepe! ¡Dios mío! ¡Pepe! (*Sale corriendo.*)

PONCIA. ¿Pero lo habéis matado?

MARTIRIO. ¡No! ¡Salió corriendo en la jaca!

BERNARDA. Fue culpa mía. Una mujer no sabe apuntar.

MAGDALENA. ¿Por qué lo has dicho entonces?

MARTIRIO. ¡Por ella! Hubiera volcado un río de sangre sobre su cabeza.

PONCIA. Maldita.

tyrant's rod. Don't take another step. No one rules me but Pepe!

MAGDALENA *enters.*

MAGDALENA. Adela!

PONCIA *and* ANGUSTIAS *appear.*

ADELA. I am his woman. (*To* ANGUSTIAS.) Is that clear? Go out there now and tell him you know. He will be master of all this house. He's waiting outside, breathing like a lion.

ANGUSTIAS. Oh, God!

BERNARDA. The gun! Where is the gun? (*She runs out.*)

AMELIA *enters upstage, looking on in terror, her head against the wall.* MARTIRIO *goes out.*

ADELA. No one will stop me! (*She starts to go out.*)

ANGUSTIAS (*restraining her*). You aren't leaving here with your body in triumph. You've stolen him! You've shamed this house!

MAGDALENA. Let her go! Somewhere where we'll never see her again!

A gunshot is heard.

BERNARDA (*entering*). Now dare to look for him!

MARTIRIO (*entering*). The end of Pepe el Romano!

ADELA. Pepe! My God! Pepe! (*She rushes out.*)

PONCIA. Have you killed him?

MARTIRIO. No. He escaped. He rode off.

BERNARDA. It was my fault. No woman can aim a gun.

MAGDALENA. Then why did you say it?

MARTIRIO. Because of her. I'd have poured a river of blood on her head!

PONCIA. You evil woman!

MAGDALENA. ¡Endemoniada!

BERNARDA. Aunque es mejor así. (*Se oye como un golpe.*) ¡Adela! ¡Adela!

PONCIA (*en la puerta*). ¡Abre!

BERNARDA. Abre. No creas que los muros defienden de la vergüenza.

CRIADA (*entrando*). ¡Se han levantado los vecinos!

BERNARDA (*en voz baja, como un rugido*). ¡Abre, porque echaré abajo la puerta!

Pausa. Todo queda en silencio.

¡Adela! (*Se retira de la puerta.*) ¡Trae un martillo!

La PONCIA *da un empujón y entra. Al entrar da un grito y sale.*

BERNARDA. ¿Qué?

PONCIA (*se lleva las manos al cuello*). ¡Nunca tengamos ese fin!

Las hermanas se echan hacia atrás. La CRIADA *se santigua.* BERNARDA *da un grito y avanza.*

PONCIA. ¡No entres!

BERNARDA. No. ¡Yo no! Pepe: irás corriendo vivo por lo oscuro de las alamedas, pero otro día caerás. ¡Descolgarla! ¡Mi hija ha muerto virgen! Llevadla a su cuarto y vestirla como si fuera doncella. ¡Nadie dirá nada! ¡Ella ha muerto virgen! Avisad que al amanecer den dos clamores las campanas.

MARTIRIO. Dichosa ella mil veces que lo pudo tener.

BERNARDA. Y no quiero llantos. La muerte hay que mirarla cara a cara. ¡Silencio! (*A otra hija.*) ¡A callar he dicho! (*A otra hija.*) Las lágrimas cuando estés sola.

MAGDALENA. You she-devil!

BERNARDA. Though it's better like this. (*A thud is heard.*) Adela! Adela!

PONCIA (*at the door*). Open the door!

BERNARDA. Open the door! Don't think the walls protect you from shame.

SERVANT (*entering*). The neighbours are getting up!

BERNARDA (*in a low, rough voice*). Open the door, or I'll break it down.

> *Pause. Everything is silent.*

Adela! (*She moves away from the door.*) Bring a hammer!

> PONCIA *pushes the door and enters. As she does so, she cries out and reappears.*

BERNARDA. What is it?

PONCIA (*putting her hands to her throat*). May we never end like that!

> *The sisters draw back. The* SERVANT *crosses herself.* BERNARDA *cries out and steps forward.*

PONCIA. Don't go in!

BERNARDA. No, I shall not! Pepe: this time you've escaped with your life, galloping off through the dark trees. But one day you will fall. Cut her down! My daughter has died a virgin! Carry her to her room and dress her like a virgin. No one will say anything! She died a virgin. Tell them the bells should ring twice at daybreak.

MARTIRIO. She was lucky to have enjoyed him!

BERNARDA. I want no weeping. One has to look death in the face. Silence! (*To another daughter.*) Be quiet, I said! (*To another daughter.*) Tears when you're alone! We

¡Nos hundiremos todas en un mar de luto! Ella, la hija menor de Bernarda Alba, ha muerto virgen. ¿Me habéis oído? Silencio, silencio he dicho. ¡Silencio!

Telón.

Día viernes 19 de junio, 1936

shall drown ourselves in a sea of mourning! She, Bernarda Alba's youngest daughter, died a virgin. Did you hear me? Silence! Silence, I said! Silence!

Curtain.

Friday 19 June, 1936

Notes

3 In the list of characters in the manuscript Lorca gives
   Angustias's age as thirty-six. This is clearly a mistake. On
   p. 27 Bernarda's observation that Angustias is thirty-nine is
   supported by a later comment from Magdalena who says,
   giving her approximate age, that she is forty. Had Lorca lived
   to see the play in production, such errors would clearly have
   been corrected. Lorca's note at the end of the list of
   characters that his play is intended to be a 'photographic
   documentary' (*documental fotográfico*) points to his desire to
   achieve a strong sense of realism in this play and the
   starkness of a black and white photograph or film. In this
   context it is interesting to bear in mind his enthusiasm for the
   cinema of his day.

5 Lorca's stage-directions are always extremely important, giving
   added emphasis to the central thrust of a scene or act. In the
   opening stage-direction here, the whiteness of the walls of
   Bernarda's house is realistic in the sense that they are painted
   white, but whiteness suggests other things too: the purity and
   virginity of Bernarda's daughters; her own concern with an
   unblemished reputation; and the monotony and sterility of the
   girls' lives. That monotony is also emphasised by the tolling
   of the bells, which point to the inescapable hold of the
   Church and of tradition upon the life of the village. The
   thick walls suggest an imprisonment which, in the case of
   Bernarda's daughters, is both physical and emotional, while
   the paintings of *unrealistic landscapes* (*paisajes inverosímiles*) evoke a
   magical world from which the women are totally excluded.

5 *making my head ache*: the literal translation of *metido entre las
   sienes*
   is 'stuck between my temples'. I have opted here for a more
   natural-sounding phrase.

5 *wailing*: the Spanish expression *gori-gori* can mean either
   'wailing', 'dirge' or 'funeral chant'.

5   *The only one her father loved*: this is the reading of the manuscript
    version. The Spanish text published by Losada in 1946, on
    which most subsequent editions were based, has *Era la única que
    quería al padre* ('the only one who loved her father'), which does
    not necessarily mean that her father loved her.

5   *sausage-jar*: *orza* is a glazed earthenware jar. This is an example
    of the way in which Lorca solidly grounds the action of the
    play in the real world of concrete things and objects.

5   *chickpeas*: *garbanzos* are dried yellow peas, extremely popular in
    Spain and frequently used in stews. They should not be
    confused with green peas or beans, as is the case in some
    translations.

7   *all she surveys*: the literal translation of *todos los que la rodean* is
    'all those who surround her'.

7   *dishes*: *vidriado* means 'glazed pottery'.

7   *to see the corpse*: *a verlo muerto* is, literally, 'to see him dead'.

7   *in this house*: *bajo estos techos* is, literally, 'under this roof'.

7   *on her own ground*: *en su dominio* has in Spanish the double
    meaning of 'territory' and 'domination'.

7   *a red-hot nail in her eyes*: *¡mal dolor de clavo le pinche en los ojos!*
    translates literally 'may the sharp pain of a nail pierce her
    eyes'.

9   *My sons work in her fields*: the fact that Poncia's sons are
    employees of Bernarda clearly gives the latter an additional
    hold over the servant, not least when we bear in mind the
    level of unemployment in rural Spain, and particularly in
    Andalusia, in the 1930s. See, for example, Raymond Carr,
    Modern Spain 1875–1980, Oxford University Press, 1985.

9   *the first husband's child*: as the only child of Bernarda's first
    marriage, Angustias would have inherited some of her father's
    money, as Amelia points out later in Act One. Why her
    stepfather should subsequently leave her more money than he
    does to his natural daughters is a matter for conjecture, not
    least when we learn from Poncia in the opening lines of the
    play that Magdalena was his favourite. See the introduction
    (p. xxxiv) on this point.

9   *This glass*: the glass from which the marks cannot be removed
    anticipates the staining of Bernarda's good name by Adela's
    misdemeanours and the local gossip which they will inevitably
    precipitate.

9   *Tronchapinos*: there appeared in the newspaper, *El Defensor de Granada*, on 11 October 1924 an item which mentioned an individual who was known locally as 'Tronchapinos' on account of the power and depth of his bass voice. 'Tronchapinos' means, literally, a 'snapper of pine trees'. Once more Lorca's choice of name is seen to be firmly grounded in local history.

11 *strain something else*: *hacía polvo yo* means 'I used to wear out'. Poncia's lewd remark typifies the earthiness of Spanish servants, particularly older women who, as Juan Antonio Bardem points out, are no longer answerable to men. See Bardem's often illuminating director's notes to his production of the play at the Teatro Goya in Madrid in 1964 (*La casa de Bernarda Alba*, Ayma, 1964, pp. 109–22).

11 *That's the way out*: literally, 'Through the door one goes to the street'. In his production notes Bardem makes the point that the lighting of the stage should be uniform except for those moments in the action when a door or a window is opened and light floods in from outside. This, of course, emphasises the existence of the world outside Bernarda's house which her daughters long to experience but cannot.

11 *the mess you've made with your feet*: *habéis dejado los pies señalados* means 'you've left your footmarks'.

11 *Floors polished with oil*: linseed or olive-oil was used to treat stone and unglazed floors in the houses of wealthier families. The 'pedestals' alluded to here probably had vases or statues placed on them.

11 *A bitter pill to swallow*: the Spanish text here translates as 'so we swallow quinine'. Quinine or sulphate of quinine is used in medicine, particularly for the treatment of malarial conditions, and has an extremely bitter taste.

11 *fine gold trim*: in Spain the coffin is traditionally lined with black or mauve material, and at one time the upper part was edged with gilt. The silk straps or 'towels' for carrying the coffin are an indication of the wealth of the Alba family.

13 *At the back of the stage*: Bardem suggests that the women enter through the door which leads to the street, allowing the sunlight to stream in before the door is closed again.

13 *The two hundred women*: in the manuscript Lorca underlined *two hundred* (*doscientas*), though such a number would have been

impossible even in an era when dramatists were not concerned about the size of the cast. He may well have intended a joke. In his Madrid production Bardem had twenty mourners in addition to Bernarda, her daughters and the servants. The manuscript also refers to Bernarda's stick, which editions before Mario Hernández's mention only at the end of the play, despite the importance of the stick as a symbol of Bernarda's authority.

15 *stop crying*: once again Magdalena is picked out as the daughter who is most upset by her father's death.

15 *the threshing*: the task of separating the grains of corn from the husk, often with a flail.

15 *small white jars*: to hand out 200 or more jars of lemonade would scarcely be a practical proposition in any production.

15 *the widower from Darajalí*: Darajalí is a hamlet in the province of Granada.

15 *pair of trousers*: *pana* is 'corduroy', the hard-wearing trousers worn by farmers and the like.

17 *Dried-up*: *recocida* means 'over-cooked' or 'eaten up inside'. Lizards are often associated with sexual desire, in which case the First Woman implies that Bernarda, now sixty years of age and a widow, is consumed by frustration.

17 *Like a twisted vine reaching out*: the image is particularly vivid. It suggests Bernarda's dry and wrinkled skin, like an old vine, as well as the deep-seated natural instinct which still burns in her ageing body.

17 *the heavenly host above you*: literally, 'the heavenly host at the head of the bed'.

17 *Saint Michael*: in Revelations 12:7, Saint Michael (San Miguel) and his angels engage in battle with the Devil, defeat him and cast him out of Heaven.

19 '*Requiem aeternam . . .*': the opening line of the Latin requiem mass.

19 *They all file out*: the mourners file out through the door to the street, Angustias through another door. The opening of the two doors simultaneously would flood the room with sunlight.

19 *caves*: the manuscript reading. Editions prior to Hernández's have 'houses' (*casas*).

19 *underskirts*: *refajos* are flannel underskirts, worn by village women over petticoats.

21   *with red and green flowers*: the flowers link Adela with Paca la
      Roseta and the harvesters, both synonymous with life and
      passion, and also with the grandmother, María Josefa, who
      dreams of passion. For a discussion of colours in the play, see
      the introduction (pp. xxx–ii).

21   *In the eight years*: the customary period of mourning for a close
      member of the family was five years. The extra three years
      are an example of Bernarda's harshness, as well, perhaps, as
      her desire to outdo the other villagers in everything.

21   *sheets*: the Spanish text has *sábanas y embozos*. The *embozo* is the
      top part of the sheet which is folded back.

21   *You can't carry tales*: another pointer to Magdalena's close
      relationship with her father.

23   *grandmother*: the manuscript reading. Editions prior to that of
      Hernández have *abuelo* (grandfather). The notion of heredity
      in relation to physical qualities and personality is not only
      very prominent in Lorca's work but is often associated with
      the concept of destiny. Thus, the Bride in *Blood Wedding* is
      said to be very similar in appearance to her mother, who, we
      are told, did not love her husband. If, therefore, María Josefa
      is like her mother in physical strength, the implication is that
      her daughter, Bernarda, could also inherit her mental state,
      and that in time Bernarda's daughters will do so too.

23   *the neighbours can see her*: this is a good example of Bernarda's
      concern with the opinion the villagers have of her. They must
      not be provided with the slightest opportunity to gossip about
      her family. Wells and water-tanks are very common indeed in
      Andalusia and the incidence of individuals drowning in them,
      both by accident and design, is considerable. Lorca's work
      contains many allusions to it. In Act Two of *Blood Wedding*,
      when the Bride has eloped with Leonardo, the Mother of the
      Bridegroom observes that a woman who felt any shame in
      such circumstances would have drowned herself. And at the
      end of the poem, 'Somnambular Ballad' ('Romance
      sonámbulo'), the despairing young woman drowns herself in
      the water-tank at the top of the house.

25   *the main door*: the *portón* is not the front door of the house
      through which the mourners have exited earlier, but a very
      large outer door in the wall which surrounds the sides and
      back of the house.

27 *the olive-grove*: olive-trees are abundant in the fertile plain or *vega* of Granada with which Lorca was so familiar. In his work the green of their leaves is a frequent symbol of fertility.

27 *suck their fingers*: I prefer to retain the literal translation of Lorca's phrase *se chupan los dedos*. The English equivalent would be 'lick their lips', but Lorca's original seems to me both stronger and more typical of the markedly physical character of his language.

27 *white and sugary*: *untuoso* means 'sticky' but can also be used to describe a sickly-sweet voice or manner.

29 *the will*: *las particiones* means, literally, the 'sharing-out' of the dead man's estate.

29 *whitewashing the courtyard*: the reference here is presumably to whitewashing the walls of the courtyard rather than the floor.

29 *without thinking*: *como un reloj* is, literally, 'like a clock', i.e. mechanically.

31 *out of the house*: *al tranco de la calle* means 'as far as the threshold'.

31 *This gossip*: Amelia is referring to the readiness of people to criticise others.

31 *sticks the knife right in*: *puñaladas* are, literally, blows or thrusts.

31 *a terrible repetition*: the suggestion is that Adelaida's fate will be similar to that of her mother and her grandmother and is already foreshadowed in the behaviour of her fiancé.

31 *Enrique Humanes*: the name is given as 'Humanas' in all the editions of the play prior to that of Mario Hernández.

33 *he'd be coming*: we discover later that it is Bernarda who has prevented Enrique from coming to court Martirio, on the grounds that he is not of her class. Martirio's description of herself waiting at her window in her nightdress establishes a link between her and Adela who, in Act Two, is described by Poncia as 'standing almost naked, with the lamp lit and the window open, when Pepe passed'. The episode contradicts Martirio's earlier claim that she would rather have nothing to do with men, pointing instead to an interest in them sharpened by growing frustration.

33 *And as ugly as sin*: Lorca's phrase, *¡Y fea como un demonio!*, means 'And ugly as a devil!'.

33 *Nothing much*: in the Spanish text Martirio's response is simply

Aquí, meaning 'We are just here', i.e. not doing anything special.

33 *spiteful gossip wasn't the fashion*: again attention is drawn to the readiness of people to malign others and thus sully their good name.

35 *It's about to strike*: the emphasis on striking clocks in Lorca's plays reveals his own concern, as he grew older, with passing time. Consider, for example, the title of his play of 1931, *When Five Years Pass*. In *The House of Bernarda Alba* the daughters are particularly conscious of life passing them by, the ticking and striking of clocks made even more apparent by the silence of the house.

35 *Pepe el Romano*: on the left bank of the river Genil, not far from Granada, is the small village of Romilla whose inhabitants are known as *romerillos* or *romanos*. This is, therefore, the place from which Pepe el Romano comes and which gives him his name. It is known that, as a child, Lorca used to visit, near Romilla, the ruins of an Arab watchtower, the Torre de Roma, which was full of toads and insects and which frightened him greatly.

35 *to ask for her hand*: *un emisario* is the emissary or third person employed by the prospective bridegroom to ask for the young woman's hand in marriage. Here we have an indication of the formality associated with courting and engagement, part of the traditional world which Bernarda upholds.

37 *her father's money*: Angustias's wealth arouses the resentment of Magdalena in particular, above all when it is revealed later on that she has been left a substantial amount of money by her stepfather at the expense of his natural daughters.

37 *just like her father did*: another pointer to the importance of heredity.

39 *my skin*: literally *las carnes*, 'my flesh'.

39 *I want to go out!*: as Act One draws to its conclusion, this phrase becomes a kind of refrain which is taken up just afterwards by Angustias – 'Mother, let me go out!' – and then by María Josefa – 'Let me go out, Bernarda!' The desperation of the women contained in the house acquires an almost operatic quality and draws attention to one of the most important aspects of Lorca's language: its musicality.

41 *the window of your room*: Adela's bedroom is not upstairs but on the ground floor facing the street (see the introduction, p. xxiii).

43   *two-faced creature! Painted doll!*: *Suavona* can mean 'sweet' in the
      sense of 'sly'.

43   *where it belongs*: *!Guárdate la lengua en la madriguera!* means 'keep
      your tongue in the burrow', therefore in the mouth.

43   *moiré dress*: moiré is a silk which has a wavy appearance
      produced by passing the material between engraved cylinders,
      which impress the design on it.

45   *eating their hearts out*: the expression *hacer polvo* means 'to
      shatter', and in this context 'breaking their hearts'.

45   *Quick curtain*: only at the end of Act One does Lorca specify a
      quick curtain. The most effective curtain would undoubtedly
      be one which descends quickly rather than curtains which
      close from the wings. In either case, though, the intention is
      to suggest the imprisonment of the women, the closing in
      upon them of the four walls of the stage. Lorca's plays were,
      of course, written for a proscenium stage. In modern theatres
      there is rarely a proscenium or a curtain.

47   *A white inner room*: this is a different room from that of Act
      One. Bardem makes the point in his production notes that it
      is essential that the action of Acts One and Two takes place
      in different rooms, for in the second act Bernarda's daughters
      must be further cut off from the outside world. At the same
      time, he suggests that the changes in the set should be
      minimal, in order to prevent unnecessary delay between the
      two acts. The 1984–85 London production, directed by Nuria
      Espert, ignored Lorca's suggestion of two different rooms,
      opting instead for a single set backed by a vast wall.

47   *sitting on low chairs, sewing*: in Lorca's work as a whole the
      image of women sewing and embroidering is a common one,
      suggesting the way in which they are imprisoned by domestic
      duties, in contrast to men. The essence of a woman's life in a
      male-dominated society is expressed vividly by the
      authoritarian figure of Don Lope in Buñuel's film *Tristana* in
      the phrase: 'La mujer honrada, pierna quebrada y en casa'
      ('A respectable woman, a broken leg and at home'), the
      Spanish equivalent of 'A woman's place is in the home'.

47   *a lizard between her breasts*: the lizard, phallic in shape, has a
      strongly sexual implication here.

47   *Open the door*: in his notes for the 1964 Madrid production,

Bardem observes that the lighting for Act Two should be constant except when a door to the outside of the house is opened, as is the case here. In the notes for José Carlos Plaza's Madrid production of 1984, it is suggested that Act Two begins at three o'clock in the afternoon, when the heat is suffocating. See *La casa de Bernarda Alba* (Los Libros del Teatro Español, 1984), which contains the text of the play and notes on the production.

49   *at the window*: the traditional Spanish courtship took place at one of the windows of the young woman's house, where the young man was, in theory, kept at a safe distance from her by the iron bars or grille on the outside of the window. If the young woman were able to use a room on the ground floor, as is the case in Lorca's play, the couple could talk quite easily. If, on the other hand, the young woman could only use an upper room, the young man was obliged to stand in the street and call up to her. He would normally arrive as it was getting dark and talk to the young woman until midnight or later, often with a break for dinner. Although the bars of the window separated the couple, they did not necessarily prevent more intimate encounters, as Poncia's subsequent account suggests.

49   *people who are always in and out of the house*: *los que van y vienen, llevan y traen* is, literally, 'those who come and go, fetch and carry' and presumably refers to tradesmen and servants.

51   *alone with a man*: see the introduction (p. xxxiii) on the possible relationship between Angustias and her stepfather. If such a relationship existed, it could have been a case of him taking advantage of her, against her will, as in the case of the Servant, and it is clearly something which she would have concealed from the other members of the family.

51   *someone with a bit of knowledge*: this is a difficult passage. Poncia seems to be saying that someone like Angustias, who is inexperienced in courtship, is bound to be tongue-tied when confronted by a man who is more experienced and more self-confident in such matters. Her description of her own first meeting at the window with her young man is a comic account of how naive both of them were.

51   *Evaristo el Colorín*: all the editions prior to Mario Hernández's have *Evaristo el Colín*. A *colorín* is a linnet, which makes Evaristo's nickname entirely appropriate.

51 *let me feel you!*: Bardem makes the point that Poncia is the
voice in the play which frequently conjures for the young
women the world of passion outside the four walls of their
mother's house.

53 *getting any fancy ideas*: the phrase *darle por otra cosa* means
'pursuing something else', by which Poncia probably means
'chasing other women'.

53 *put his eye out*: *tuerto*, literally, 'blind in one eye'.

53 *something to me*: *me dijo no sé qué cosa* means 'he said I don't
know what'. The implication is that it was something uncouth
and unrepeatable, as a result of which she took her revenge.

53 *the rolling-pin*: *la mano del almirez* means 'the end of the pestle'.
Poncia uses the pestle and mortar to crush cooking
ingredients. I have chosen to substitute an implement which is
more familiar in British kitchens.

53 *sick*: Adela is devastated by the news that Pepe el Romano,
whom she so desires, is to marry Angustias. Her sickness is
therefore emotional, but it is likely that she is also suffering
the early symptoms of pregnancy. Certainly, sufficient time
has passed between the ending of Act One and the beginning
of Act Two for Adela to have started meeting Pepe el
Romano in secret. The notes to José Carlos Plaza's Madrid
production suggest that one month has passed, but Adela has
been meeting Pepe even before this (see note to p. 101, '*And
other things*').

53 *with just a wall between you*: Martirio, sleeping in the next room
to Adela, is in a position to watch her every move and
undoubtedly spies on her during the night – as in Mario
Camus's film version of the play. There is much in this
second act to suggest that Adela is indeed leaving the house
at night to meet Pepe.

55 *the lace*: the lace is for Angustias's wedding-sheets. In Act One
we are told that Pepe el Romano will 'soon be sending
someone to ask for her hand'. The fact that in Act Two
preparations are being made for the wedding is another
indication that some time has passed between the two acts.

55 *my bright eyes*: literally, 'my eyes, which are clear'.

55 *She follows me everywhere*: presumably Martirio did not behave
in this way until she became aware of Adela's nocturnal
activities.

57 *Where do you go at night when you get up?*: a clear suggestion that Adela not only stands at her window, as Poncia observes a moment later, but that she also goes out of her bedroom.

57 *the window open*: since Adela's bedroom is on the ground floor, Pepe el Romano, on his way to see Angustias, described by Poncia as old and by Magdalena as a 'stick wrapped in a dress at twenty', would pass within touching distance of the 'almost naked' Adela. Poncia's words brilliantly evoke the erotic charge of the situation.

59 *to be disgraced*: *mancharme de vieja* means, literally, 'to be stained in my old age', i.e. the stain of dishonour. In her regard for good name and reputation Poncia, though less extreme than Bernarda, can be said to be as much a traditionalist.

59 *this fire*: the heat and flame of passion within Adela echoes the fire which Poncia has earlier described as 'coming out of the ground'. In Lorca's work natural passions are constantly linked to the irresistible forces of Nature, thereby evoking their inevitability and the powerlessness of individuals to resist them.

59 *drinking his blood*: one is tempted, perhaps, to think of vampirism, but in Lorca's work as a whole blood is synonymous with passion. So in *Blood Wedding*, Act Three, Scene One, the three Woodcutters describe the passion of the Bride and Leonardo:

> FIRST WOODCUTTER. They were deceiving each other. In the end the blood was strongest.
> THIRD WOODCUTTER. The blood!
> FIRST WOODCUTTER. You have to follow the blood's path.

61 *Not a word!*: *¡chitón!* means 'shush!'

61 *to flaunt myself*: Martirio is perfectly aware that, as Poncia has suggested earlier, Adela stands at her window whenever Pepe el Romano comes to court Angustias.

61 *I could never dress mine in it*: all the allusions to the lace point to Bernarda's wealth. The fact that Poncia could never dress her children in it is an indication of her comparative poverty, bringing to mind the Servant's bitter complaint in Act One about 'those of us who live in huts of mud'. See the introduction, p. xxv, on Lorca's social awareness in this play.

61 *brats*: *monigotes* really means 'rag dolls', hence 'ragamuffins' or 'brats'.

61 *a bit of a scuffle*: *porrazos* means 'blows'. Presumably the 'brats' are fighting amongst themselves or being smacked. In either case the scene is lively.

61 *convent*: a sarcastic reference not only to the chastity of the young women but also, perhaps, to the 'Mother Superior' who rules their lives.

61 *to work*: editions prior to that of Mario Hernández have *del trabajo*, 'from work', rather than *al trabajo*, 'to work', but the harvesters are clearly returning to the fields.

63 *Each class does what it must*: Magdalena, the eldest daughter, shares many of her mother's traditional views.

63 *The harvesters came yesterday*: the annual influx of hired workers was something with which Lorca was clearly very familiar, both on his father's estate and on the estates of neighbouring landowners.

63 *green eyes*: the colour not only links the young man to the world of flourishing Nature but also to Adela with her green dress and her fan with its red and green flowers. Quite how Poncia could have seen the colour of the young man's eyes when, as she says, she saw the harvesters 'from a long way off' is a bit of a mystery.

63 *the greatest punishment*: an echo in a different context of Segismundo's lines in Act One of Calderón's *Life is a Dream*, when he observes that man's greatest crime is simply to have been born. This is a play which Lorca knew very well.

65 *carrañacas*: rustic percussive instruments.

65 *knows her own heart*: literally, 'knows her things' or 'affairs'.

65 *Open your doors and windows*: the words evoke a world of freedom and openness, in contrast to the closed doors and windows of Bernarda's house.

65 *roses*: the allusion to roses evokes the red flowers of Adela's fan and therefore links her once more to the world of vibrant and flourishing Nature.

65 *they'll give it a push*: further evidence that Adela's bedroom is on the ground floor, facing the street.

67 *I might have imagined it*: all the editions prior to Mario Hernández's have *puede ser un barrunto mío* ('it could be a conjecture of mine'). Hernández has *Puede ser un volunto mío*. I

have not been able to find the word *volunto* in any dictionary.

69 *silver Saint Bartholomew*: one of the twelve apostles. In Andalusia he is associated with good looks, hence Amelia's sarcastic remark, though elsewhere Pepe el Romano is said to be the best-looking young man in the area. 'Silver' could refer to a silver picture frame.

69 *Any one of us, but not me!*: the clear suggestion is that, if Martirio is aware of Adela's secret meetings with Pepe el Romano, Adela is also aware of Martirio's interest in him.

71 *This comes from not keeping you on a shorter leash*: the Spanish original, *Esto tiene no ataros más cortas*, means 'This is from not tying you shorter'.

71 *But I shall haunt you all in your dreams*: *¡Pero me vais a soñar!* means 'You are going to dream about me', i.e. have nightmares.

71 *you sly creature! Nothing but a troublemaker!*: Lorca's phrase *mosca muerta* means 'hypocrite' or 'slyboots'. As for the phrase *Sembradura de vidrios* ('Land sown with glass'), it is common to all editions and is possibly an error for *Sembradora de vidrios* ('Sower of glass'), i.e. someone who creates problems for others.

73 *jokes*: *juegos* is, literally, 'games'.

73 *You are both mad*: Magdalena here, and Amelia in the next line, are addressing Adela and Martirio, as the second-person plural form of the verbs makes clear.

73 *let the current take them*: the precise meaning of Adela's words is not clear. She may be referring to her own boldness in flaunting herself at the window, though this is unlikely in the circumstances. It seems more likely that she is hinting at untoward behaviour on Martirio's part in order to divert suspicion from herself.

73 *your land and your orchards*: a *marjal* is a measurement of land, roughly equivalent to an acre.

75 *a hundred miles*: literally, 'a hundred leagues'. A league in Spain is about 5,572 metres.

77 *prone to falling in love*: *enamoradiza* means 'romantically inclined'.

77 *your protection*: Poncia's origins remain a mystery in the play, for we have only Bernarda's remarks as pointers to anything that might be other than normal. Poncia's 'Don't remind me!', as well as her reference to Bernarda's 'protection',

suggest that there is something disreputable in her background and Bernarda hints below that her mother was a whore.

79 *it's hard for people to go against their true nature*: in *Blood Wedding*, Act Three, Scene One, the Second Woodcutter observes of the Bride and Leonardo: 'You have to follow your instinct. They were right to run away.' On this point see the introduction (p. xxxviii–xl).

79 *even Nature herself would agree*: the Spanish has *y hasta al aire*, i.e. 'even the air'.

79 *tear you to pieces*: *te tendría que arañar* means 'I would have to scratch you', but a rather stronger expression is clearly required.

79 *It won't come to that*: the expression *no llegará la sangre al río* ('the blood won't reach the river') commonly refers to disputes, meaning that things will not reach the stage feared or anticipated.

79 *fly to the rooftops*: *se te subirán al tejado* means 'they will go up to the roof', but the image of birds flying is clearly implied and underlines the notion of freedom.

79 *fought the good fight!*: *gasté sabrosa pimienta*, literally, 'I used tasty pepper'.

79 *smitten*: *picado*, 'stimulated' or 'spurred on'.

81 *the oxen*: *yunta* is the 'yoke', the meaning therefore 'oxen yoked together'.

81 *to show myself*: a virtual admission that Martirio was not lying in bed but that she was standing by her window, careful not to reveal herself.

81 *facing the alley-way*: Adela's room seems to be at the side of the house. So, in Act One, four of the young women watch Pepe el Romano from Adela's room when he has turned the corner, i.e. turned off the main street, which Angustias's room faces. The side-street also allows Adela to speak to Pepe with less risk of being seen.

81 *Take care you don't discover the truth!*: an ironical allusion on Poncia's part to Bernarda's earlier remark: 'You creep up to fill me with bad dreams. I don't want to know.'

81 *I'm as hard as flint*: *se encontrarán con mi pedernal*, 'they will come up against my flint'.

83 *No one tells me what to do*: the phrase *Nadie me traiga ni me lleve*

means 'Let no one fetch or take me', i.e. 'Let no one push me around'.

83 *Find out what's happening!*: Bernarda, who is so anxious that no one should know of and be able to gossip about what is happening in her own house, is among the first to want to know what has happened outside it. She is very much part of that inward-looking mentality which is so typical of small towns and villages.

83 *displaying yourselves at the windows*: the Spanish is very concise here, the adjective *ventaneras* describing women who are forever at the window, eager to see and be seen.

83 *to the courtyard!*: the courtyard or *patio* is at the back of the house, away from the street.

83 *gets there first*: the phrase *se adelanta* ('pushing oneself forward') is, it has been suggested, associated with the name Adela. On the symbolism of the names in the play, see J. Rubia Barcia, 'El realismo "mágico" de *La casa de Bernarda Alba*', pp. 388–9; L. González del Valle, *La tragedia en el teatro de Unamuno, Valle-Inclán y García Lorca*, p. 163; and Robert Lima, *The Theater of García Lorca*, p. 271.

83 *Never!*: Martirio's *De ninguna* means 'No way' ('De ninguna manera').

83 *I saw how he embraced you!*: Adela and Pepe el Romano may, of course, embrace through the bars of the window, but this would run the risk of someone seeing them. It is quite likely, therefore, that Adela slips out of the house to meet Pepe elsewhere, and that Martirio follows them and spies on their love-making – as in Mario Camus's film version of the play.

83 *dragged by a rope*: in Act Three, Scene Two, of *Blood Wedding*, the Bride describes how her passion for Leonardo drags her along in a similar way, which points to her helplessness in that situation: 'Your son was my ambition and I haven't deceived him, but the other one's arm dragged me like a wave from the sea, like the butt of a mule, and would always have dragged me . . .'

85 *And to hide her shame*: if Poncia is herself illegitimate, it is a masterly stroke on Lorca's part to have her, rather than anyone else, describe the victimisation of a young woman who has given birth to such a child. In these circumstances Poncia's speech should acquire in performance an extraordinary power.

85 *clutching her stomach*: this seems to confirm the earlier pointers
to the fact that Adela is pregnant.

87 *bathed in blue*: the bluish effect is, in part, created by the light
of the moon on the white walls. The colour blue in Lorca's
theatre is frequently associated with death, as indeed is the
moon itself. In a brilliantly dramatic scene in Act One of
When Five Years Pass, the Dead Child and the Dead Cat enter
as '*The light fades and the stage is filled with a blue glow*', and in
Act Three, Scene One, of *Blood Wedding*, the Moon appears
as '*The stage takes on an intense blue light . . .*'

87 *the inner courtyard*: if the location for Act Two is further
removed from the outside world than Act One, this is also
true of *the inner courtyard*. Although the sky may be visible to
the characters, Bardem suggests that the audience should not
be able to see it. Instead, the walls of the set should be high
in order to create the feeling that these women are at the
bottom of a well of bitterness, the beauty of the sky and of
Nature in general beyond their reach. In the notes for José
Carlos Plaza's 1984 Madrid production, it is suggested that
the time-interval between the action of Acts Two and Three
is three days.

87 *Prudencia*: in the introduction to his edition of the play,
Ramsden sets out his reservations against regarding the play
as a perfect work (*La casa de Bernarda Alba*, Manchester
University Press, 1983, pp. lv–lix). One thing which
Prudencia's visit does, of course, suggest is the obsession with
family name and reputation in houses other than Bernarda's,
but her visit certainly contradicts the general thrust of
Poncia's statement in Act One that 'Since Bernarda's father
died, no one has ever set foot in this house', and, shortly
afterwards, Bernarda's own assertion about the neighbours:
'Let it be years before you cross my threshold again!' Had he
lived and worked further on the play, it seems likely that
Lorca would have eliminated such contradictions.

89 *The stallion*: the image is not quite precise because, in
Bernarda's house, those who are locked up are women.
Nevertheless, the notion of repressed instinct desperately
seeking to break out is powerfully conveyed by this incident,
and it is also an ominous pointer to the events which lie
ahead.

89   *the best stable*: in one sense this is a further indication of
      Bernarda's wealth, but it is also a sarcastic reference on
      Poncia's part to the daughters whom Bernarda has previously
      described as being too good for any of the locals.

89   *to roll in the straw*: the words are ironic in the light of Adela's
      activities with Pepe el Romano in the stable.

89   *before he brings the walls on top of us*: again there is considerable
      and unintentional irony in Bernarda's words, for what is true
      of the stallion will prove to be true of Pepe el Romano who
      will eventually, if not literally, bring down the walls upon the
      entire household.

91   *to make a formal request in the next three days*: *a pedirla* means 'to
      ask for her'. In Act One Magdalena observes of Angustias: 'I
      think he'll soon be sending someone to ask for her hand'. In
      Act Two lace arrives for the wedding-sheets, and in Act
      Three Angustias is wearing the engagement ring. Here,
      Bernarda's allusion to a 'formal request' must refer to the last
      step in the process, whereby the final permission for marriage
      is sought by the young man.

91   *as God wills them!*: *como Dios dispone*, 'as God disposes', the
      reference being to the Spanish proverb, 'Man proposes, God
      disposes'.

91   *sixteen thousand reales*: a *real* was a coin worth 25 céntimos, one
      quarter of a peseta. 16,000 reales were therefore 4,000 pesetas,
      which in the 1930s would have represented a considerable
      amount. Today it would be about £24.

93   *Bells are heard in the distance*: bells are heard at the beginning of
      Acts One and Three, and at the end of Act Three Bernarda
      requests that 'the bells should ring twice at daybreak'. Their
      presence in the play underlines the extent to which the lives
      of the characters are dominated by traditional forces, of
      which the Catholic Church is a powerful element. A
      comparison may be made with Luis Buñuel's film, *Tristana*, in
      which the tolling of church bells in the opening sequence has
      similar symbolism.

93   *the main door*: the *portón* (see note to p. 25 above) is the very
      large door in the outer wall which surrounds the sides and
      back of the house. Adela knows that Pepe is likely to be
      lurking there. She will either open the door to let him in so
      that he can hide in the stable, or he will climb the wall.

93   *respectable appearance*: *buena fachada*, a 'good façade' or external
     appearance. The contrast between what one appears to be
     and what one is, which is closely connected with the notion
     of honour, has been a preoccupation of Spanish writers from
     the Middle Ages to the present day. One of the best
     examples of it occurs in the sixteenth-century picaresque
     novel, *Lazarillo de Tormes*, in which the starving 'gentleman',
     for the sake of his 'honour' or reputation, presents to the
     world at large an image of refinement and elegance.

95   *You shouldn't ask him*: Bernarda evokes a world in which
     women have virtually no freedom. It is worth remembering
     that in 1931 the Constitution of the Second Republic
     contained clauses which were designed to allow women
     considerably greater freedom, including equality in marriage
     and the right to divorce if the marriage proved to be
     unworkable. Clearly, this was not a situation which found
     favour with many Spanish men, with the Church or the
     Right. During the long dictatorship which followed the
     triumph of the Right in the Civil War the inferior position of
     women was soon re-established.

95   *you aren't strong*: if, as is often suggested, Angustias's health is
     poor, Pepe el Romano must be aware of the possibility that
     she could die in childbirth, as a result of which he would
     inherit her money. The world of human relationships which
     the play depicts is, to say the least, bleak.

97   *cricked her neck*: this line supports Bardem's suggestion that the
     audience should not be able to see the sky on account of the
     height of the walls.

97   '*Blessed Santa Barbara* . . .': according to legend, Saint Barbara
     was the daughter of a pagan father who, to protect her from
     the corruption of the world, confined her in a tower. When
     he returned from a journey and discovered that she had not
     only escaped but become a Christian, he killed her but was
     himself then killed by lightning. In Spain the traditional
     rhyme quoted by Adela became an invocation for protection
     against lightning and sudden death. The notion that stars are
     divine writing in the sky is a common one. Here Adela is
     merely fascinated by the beauty of the shooting star and
     unaware that Santa Barbara protects against sudden death;
     just as Santa Barbara defied her father only to meet her end,

Adela's fate will be similar. See also Judith M. Bull, '"Santa Bárbara" and *La casa de Bernarda Alba*', pp. 117–23.

97 *dozed off*: *Está en el primer sueño* is, literally, 'in the first stage of sleep'.

99 *Martirio takes a drink of water*: Martirio and Adela are both portrayed as thirsty in the course of this third act, their thirst in relation to water another form of their thirst for Pepe el Romano.

99 *the stable-yard*: Martirio's behaviour clearly implies that she suspects the story of Pepe el Romano accompanying his mother to the city to be merely a cover for his secret liaison with Adela.

99 *there's nothing going on*: *no hay un sí ni un no*, 'there isn't a yes or a no'.

101 *there is no meat to bite on*: a good example of the hard, physical nature of much of Lorca's imagery.

101 *What time do you want me to call you?*: the reading in the manuscript is *¿A qué hora quiere que la llame?*, while all editions prior to Mario Hernández's have *¿A qué hora quieres que te llame?* In the latter the second-person familiar form of the verb is used, which is the form in which Poncia always addresses Bernarda, while in the manuscript the third-person polite form of the verb is employed, the form in which the Servant addresses her. In his edition of the play, Ramsden suggests that the line was probably intended to be spoken by the Servant. He also points out that a line given in the manuscript to Amelia early in Act Two – 'I thought so too' ('A mí también me pareció') – is more likely to have been spoken by Martirio.

101 *And other things*: this revelation makes Adela's desperation much more comprehensible. There is again a parallel with the Bride in *Blood Wedding* who, several years before the events dramatised in the play, had had a relationship with Leonardo. Their sexual attraction to each other, like that of Adela to Pepe, proves impossible to withstand and leads to their elopement.

103 *Things have already gone too far*: in Act Three in particular, Poncia and the Servant have a role not unlike that of the Chorus in Greek tragedy, for they both impart information and create a considerable sense of foreboding. The influence

of classical drama on Lorca should not be forgotten; it
would have been reinforced by ambitious open-air
productions of classical plays, such as Seneca's *Medea*, which
he would have been able to see in Madrid in the early
1930s. The very title, *The House of Bernarda Alba*, has a rather
classical ring in its suggestion of a household and a dynasty.
In *Blood Wedding* and *Yerma* the chorus takes the form of
songs and ritualistic chanting, but in *The House of Bernarda
Alba* the greater degree of realism which Lorca sought
required that the role of chorus be used in a rather different
way through the exchanges of Poncia and the Servant.

103   *watching all the time*: Pepe el Romano has by this time had
the effect of arousing the desires, as well as the envy, of all
the daughters.

103   *white petticoat*: the contrast between the whiteness of the
petticoats and the darkness of the night is considerable in
this act and illustrates in part Lorca's indication that the play
should have the quality of a 'photographic documentary'.
But if the white/black contrast is particularly strong here, it
is also present to a lesser degree in the first two acts.

105   *Little lamb, my baby*: María Josefa's song alludes to Bethlehem
and the birth of Christ, while her own name evokes both
Mary and Joseph. In contrast to the bond of love which
should unite mother and child, and the values embodied in
Christianity, María Josefa sees in her own daughter,
Bernarda, and in her grand-daughter, Magdalena, only the
savagery of wild animals. In the evocation of the seashore
there is that suggestion of and longing for freedom and
escape which is evident elsewhere in the play in allusions to
the fields, to open windows and doors, and to the wish to go
out.

107   *face of a martyr*: see the introduction (p. xxix) on the
symbolism of some of the characters' names.

107   *the waves*: the sea, teeming with life, is a traditional symbol of
fertility, and in this sense María Josefa's speech contrasts very
strongly indeed with the sterility of Bernarda Alba's
household. The allusions to whiteness also link María Josefa
to Adela in particular, who, as the earlier stage-direction
indicates, is dressed '*in a white petticoat and bodice*'.

107   *till I'm past the fields? I don't want fields*: editions prior to Mario

Hernández's have 'al campo? Yo quiero campo' ('to the fields? I want fields'). Lorca's manuscript reading suggests that, although María Josefa desires the freedom provided by open spaces, she longs even more for houses with open doors and windows where people are at peace.

109 *I've seen death under this roof*: the line suggests a marked contrast to what is indicated by the name of the house's owner, 'Alba', which evokes dawn, and the light and optimism associated with it.

111 *hide my head in shame*: *Déjame decirlo con la cabeza fuera de los embozos* means, literally, 'Let me say it with my head outside the sheets'. The *embozo* is the top part of the sheet which is turned back.

111 *pomegranate*: this is another good example of Lorca's highly tactile imagery. One can imagine a pomegranate falling to the ground and splitting open to reveal its reddish interior. The pomegranate is a traditional symbol of fertility.

111 *let her drown*: there are various allusions in the play to allowing oneself to be taken by the current. But if the natural course is to follow one's instinct, this can also prove to be dangerous. In this context, then, the image of water, be it river or sea, suggests not only something fertile and life-giving, but also something full of risk. Unlike Poncia, who would turn her back so she cannot see the tide (p. 101), Adela would rather go with it.

111 *the crown of thorns*: Adela sees herself as a Christ-like martyr pursued by hypocritical enemies. Lorca, hounded and persecuted by those who detested his homosexuality, must sometimes have seen himself in a similar light. In Scene Four of Lorca's homosexual play, *The Public*, the stage is dominated by a suffering male figure: '*Centre stage, a bed, upright, and facing downstage, like a primitive painting; on it, a red naked man, with a crown of blue thorns.*' See the translation of the play by Henry Livings in *Lorca Plays: Three*, Methuen, 1994.

113 *a wild stallion*: un caballo encabritado, 'a rearing stallion'.

113 *God must have abandoned me*: an echo of Christ's words on the cross. Adela now feels herself to be totally alone, as well as devoid of any feelings of love or compassion towards her family.

113 *a thunderbolt between my fingers!*: in Greek mythology the

supreme deity Zeus (the Roman Jupiter) was the god of rain,
thunder, snow and the sky. He presided on Mount Olympus
and his particular attributes were the eagle and the
thunderbolt, the latter employed to take revenge on those
who angered him.

113 *my jailer*: an echo of earlier allusions to prison, chains and
     convent.

115 *a lion*: this suggests both physical strength and good looks.
     To that extent we are reminded of Leonardo in *Blood
     Wedding*, his name – 'burning lion' – suggestive of similar
     attributes.

115 *the gun*: Lorca had the good sense to have the gun offstage.
     The appearance of Bernarda on stage carrying a shot-gun or
     rifle would have a comic rather than dramatic effect.

117 *Bernarda cries out and steps forward*: the important point here is
     that Bernarda's self-control should break for only a moment
     – as happens in the film directed by Mario Camus.

117 *the bells should ring twice*: traditionally in Spain two bells toll
     for the dead.

119 *Silence!*: Bernarda's first word in the play is also her last.
     This, in conjunction with the reference to the bells, whose
     tolling opens the play, gives the action a circular structure
     which underlines the notion of enclosure and imprisonment.

Questions for further study

1   What picture is conveyed of the village in which the Alba family lives and what impression is given of the moral and social values which the villagers share?

2   Why do you think that Lorca subtitled the play 'A Drama of Women in the Villages of Spain'?

3   To what extent do Bernada Alba's daughters differ from each other in their attitudes and aspirations? How does this affect the drama?

4   Can Bernarda Alba be seen as in any way a sympathetic individual?

5   'The clash between passion and frustration – Lorca's constant preoccupation – lies at the heart of this play.' Discuss.

6   How does the imagery in the play evoke the opposing notions of sterility and vitality?

7   Discuss the importance of the theme of honour and reputation in *The House of Bernarda Alba*.

8   Which aspects of Lorca's play do you regard as relevant to a modern audience? Do you think the attitudes and values portrayed are now outdated and therefore irrelevant?

9   To what extent do the atmosphere and attitudes suggested in the play reflect the clash between left- and right-wing politics in Spain of the time?

10   'Many great plays are largely autobiographical.' Discuss Lorca's play in terms of his personal life.

11   Lorca described *The House of Bernarda Alba* as a 'photographic documentary'. Show what he meant by this.

12   Assess the importance of symbolism and imagery in *The House of Bernarda Alba*.

13   Discuss the view that, even if Lorca places the events and characters of his play in a specific Andalusian setting, they soon acquire a universal resonance.

14   To what extent can *The House of Bernarda Alba* be regarded as a tragedy?

15 If you were staging the play, what kind of approach would best accord with Lorca's intentions? Or would you wish to reinterpret it and if so why and how?

16 Choose a particular role in the play and suggest how that role might best be played.

17 'What this magnificent play shows is how realism can be elevated to the poetic level' (Michael Billington, *Guardian*, 14 January 1987). Discuss.

18 Discuss Lorca's use in *The House of Bernarda Alba* of the theatrical elements which constitute 'total theatre'.

19 Evaluate the difficulties which a British director faces in staging *The House of Bernarda Alba*.

20 What do you consider to be the principal characteristics of Lorca's dramatic language?

Bloomsbury Methuen Drama Student Editions

Jean Anouilh *Antigone* • John Arden *Serjeant Musgrave's Dance*
Alan Ayckbourn *Confusions* • Aphra Behn *The Rover* • Edward Bond
Lear • *Saved* • Bertolt Brecht *The Caucasian Chalk Circle* • *Fear and
Misery in the Third Reich* • *The Good Person of Szechwan* • *Life of Galileo* •
Mother Courage and her Children • *The Resistible Rise of Arturo Ui* • *The
Threepenny Opera* • Anton Chekhov *The Cherry Orchard* • *The Seagull* •
Three Sisters • *Uncle Vanya* • Caryl Churchill *Serious Money* • *Top Girls*
• Shelagh Delaney *A Taste of Honey* • Euripides *Elektra* • *Medea* •
Dario Fo *Accidental Death of an Anarchist* • Michael Frayn *Copenhagen*
• John Galsworthy *Strife* • Nikolai Gogol *The Government Inspector* •
Robert Holman *Across Oka* • Henrik Ibsen *A Doll's House* • *Ghosts* •
Hedda Gabler • Charlotte Keatley *My Mother Said I Never Should* •
Bernard Kops *Dreams of Anne Frank* • Federico García Lorca *Blood
Wedding* • *Doña Rosita the Spinster* (bilingual edition) • *The House of
Bernarda Alba* • (bilingual edition) • *Yerma* (bilingual edition) • David
Mamet *Glengarry Glen Ross* • *Oleanna* • Patrick Marber *Closer* • John
Marston *Malcontent* • Martin McDonagh *The Lieutenant of Inishmore* •
Joe Orton *Loot* • Luigi Pirandello *Six Characters in Search of an Author*
• Mark Ravenhill *Shopping and F***ing* • Willy Russell *Blood Brothers*
• *Educating Rita* • Sophocles *Antigone* • *Oedipus the King* • Wole
Soyinka *Death and the King's Horseman* • Shelagh Stephenson *The
Memory of Water* • August Strindberg *Miss Julie* • J. M. Synge *The
Playboy of the Western World* • Theatre Workshop *Oh What a Lovely
War* Timberlake Wertenbaker *Our Country's Good* • Arnold Wesker
The Merchant • Oscar Wilde *The Importance of Being Earnest* •
Tennessee Williams *A Streetcar Named Desire* • *The Glass Menagerie*

Bloomsbury Methuen Drama Modern Classics

Jean Anouilh *Antigone* • Brendan Behan *The Hostage* • Robert Bolt
A Man for All Seasons • Edward Bond *Saved* • Bertolt Brecht *The
Caucasian Chalk Circle* • *Fear and Misery in the Third Reich* • *The Good
Person of Szechwan* • *Life of Galileo* • *The Messingkauf Dialogues* •
Mother Courage and Her Children • *Mr Puntila and His Man Matti* •
The Resistible Rise of Arturo Ui • *Rise and Fall of the City of
Mahagonny* • *The Threepenny Opera* • Jim Cartwright *Road* • *Two &
Bed* • Caryl Churchill *Serious Money* • *Top Girls* • Noël Coward
Blithe Spirit • *Hay Fever* • *Present Laughter* • *Private Lives* • *The Vortex* •
Shelagh Delaney *A Taste of Honey* • Dario Fo *Accidental Death of an
Anarchist* • Michael Frayn *Copenhagen* • Lorraine Hansberry *A
Raisin in the Sun* • Jonathan Harvey *Beautiful Thing* • David Mamet
Glengarry Glen Ross • *Oleanna* • *Speed-the-Plow* • Patrick Marber
Closer • *Dealer's Choice* • Arthur Miller *Broken Glass* • Percy Mtwa,
Mbongeni Ngema, Barney Simon *Woza Albert!* • Joe Orton
Entertaining Mr Sloane • *Loot* • *What the Butler Saw* • Mark Ravenhill
*Shopping and F***ing* • Willy Russell *Blood Brothers* • *Educating Rita* •
Stags and Hens • *Our Day Out* • Jean-Paul Sartre *Crime Passionnel* •
Wole Soyinka • *Death and the King's Horseman* • Theatre Workshop
Oh, What a Lovely War • Frank Wedekind • *Spring Awakening* •
Timberlake Wertenbaker *Our Country's Good*

Printed in the USA
CPSIA information can be obtained
at www.ICGtesting.com
LVHW022138221024
794413LV00008B/258

9 780713 686777